SO-DGG-972

The Legal
Resource
Directory

Your Guide to Help,
Hotlines & Hot Web Sites

©1997

Project Director: Theresa Meehan Rudy
Editor: Richard Hébert
Graphics & Production: Walton-Thomas International (Joe García),
David Bell
Substantial Assistance Provided By: Edward Tannouse, Robyn Goldman,
Lina Kee and Bob Weiss.

Every effort has been made to make sure the information in *The Legal Resource Directory* is as accurate as possible, but as with all directory information, addresses, telephone numbers and web site URLs change without notice. If a piece of information has changed, and you would like to notify us about it for the next edition, please use the form at the end of this book.

© 1997, HALT, Inc., 1612 K St., NW, Ste. 510, Washington, DC 20006

First Edition: November, 1997
ISBN 0-910073-23-6

Also by HALT:

Using a Lawyer
Wills
Real Estate
Everyday Contracts
Small Claims Court
The Smart Consumer
Using the Law Library
Legal Rights for Seniors
The Easy Way to Probate
You, Your Family & the Law
If You Want to Sue a Lawyer
Your Guide to Living and Other Trusts

TABLE OF CONTENTS

INTRODUCTION

Over the years, HALT has fielded thousands of calls from people who want to take charge of their legal affairs but need information, direction or referrals.

Unlike other areas of consumer interest—in which information about products, services and prices abounds—the consumer is often in the dark about how to handle even the simplest legal matters. For the most part, lawyers would like to keep it that way, because it means consumers will continue to turn to them for answers. For many, that's not always necessary, advisable, or even feasible.

The situation is improving. Many routine legal tasks, such as writing a will, filing for bankruptcy or getting an uncontested divorce, can now be done without a lawyer's help. Do-it-yourself legal publications and forms are making it possible. But, what about the myriad legal concerns and issues for which a fill-in-the-blank legal form is not the answer?

That is why HALT has prepared *The Legal Resource Directory*. This book tells you who to contact to get answers to a variety of everyday legal issues and concerns, whether you're having a problem with a local business, need to file a complaint against a lawyer, want to report fraud or abuse of a government program, need help selecting a hospice or any of hundreds of other situations that have legal implications. Answers to these "How do I do it?" questions can be found in these pages. Many of the resources listed include contact names, addresses, toll free telephone numbers and facsimile numbers.

As with any self-respecting resource book of today, *The Legal Resource Directory* includes a wealth of Internet resources. Each chapter ends with a "Web Sites" section. The Internet is truly changing the way we get information and communicate with each other. Almost any question you can think of asking has an answer on the Net. And on most sites, you can download the forms you'll need for simple legal transactions.

HOW TO USE THIS BOOK

We suggest you browse through the entire book first to familiarize yourself with the range of resources we have included, then review the sections that have the specific information you're looking for when you need it. Here's what you'll find inside:

Chapter 1 focuses on the legal needs of seniors. It lists legal hotlines, government programs and state and national organizations that distribute literature, make referrals or act as advocates on behalf of seniors. And, of course, it gives you over a dozen Internet addresses tailored to seniors' needs.

Chapter 2 puts you in touch with your government. It tells you how to contact federal agencies, including the Internal Revenue Service, the Social Security Administration, the Patent and Trademark Office and the Department of Veterans Affairs. It lists the offices of all 50 governors, attorneys general and secretaries of state plus both federal and state government agency web sites.

Chapter 3 helps you take better control of your consumer and credit-related problems by putting you in touch with private sector and government offices that deal with these problems. Additional information can be found about "consumers rights" on various web sites listed at the end of this section.

Chapter 4 offers car owners information, resources and help in purchasing, selling and repairing new and used cars.

Chapter 5 tells where to go to file a complaint against an attorney, whether you're having a fee dispute or a communication problem, or suspect an ethics violation or outright theft. The web site list in this section connects you to online state bar associations and private sites interested in compiling information about lawyers, both good and bad.

Chapter 6 "Alternative Legal Resources," has information on getting your legal needs met through pre-paid legal plans, legal advice telephone lines, independent paralegals and advocacy and support groups. Its list of web sites takes you to information about legal research tools on the Internet geared to both lawyers and nonlawyers, and information for pro se litigants.

1

HELP FOR SENIORS & THEIR FAMILIES

The senior population is growing rapidly. In 1996, almost 4 million Americans were 85 years old or older. By the middle of the next century, projections range from more than 9 million to more than 30 million seniors in that age group—and close to a million centenarians.

As with the rest of society, these seniors increasingly find themselves caught up in the complexities of modern life. Everything has become so fast paced, so complex and, yes, legalistic. The rules of government programs can be daunting and the laws that regulate a wide variety of seniors' concerns—from getting government benefits to planning their estates—can be confusing, even intimidating.

But there is good news, too! Seniors (or their guardians) can find lots of help for handling legal matters. This chapter identifies those resources and contacts that address the special needs of seniors. Here you will find information about Social Security, Medicare, Medicaid, housing for seniors, home care, hospice care and more. Many of the organizations listed in this chapter operate both toll free telephone lines and web sites.

If you're a senior or someone who is taking care of an elder citizen, a word of advice: don't limit yourself to this chapter. Other chapters also can take you to resources that apply to seniors' concerns, even though they are not specifically targeted to them. It's only logical: senior citizens are like everyone else in many respects, only older. What concerns a 30- or 50-year-old very likely will be an issue for an 80-year-old as well. For example, help resolving a consumer dispute (Chapter 3), finding a do-it-yourself law book (Chapter 6), or getting help from a government agency (Chapter 2) is important to everyone, young or old.

It's worth mentioning here, too, that seniors (or their caregivers) need to be particularly aware of scam artists. According to the U.S. Senate Special Committee on Aging, seniors are considered "easy marks" who are often singled out for abuse by criminals and unethical merchants. The marketplace sectors in which seniors are most likely to be victimized include home repairs, medical insurance, estate planning, nursing-home care, home health-care, housing and automobile sales and repairs. The best way to avoid becoming a victim is to use common sense, know your rights, and *know who to contact if you suspect fraud*. The first of these is up to you. We hope this book helps with the other two.

SOCIAL SECURITY

Social Security is administered by the Social Security Administration (SSA), an agency of the U.S. Department of Health and Human Services. This program was created by federal law; the rules of eligibility are the same in every state.

Social Security is actually three income programs in one. Although most people think of Social Security as a retirement program, it is also both a disability insurance program and an annuity program for dependents and survivors. You or your family may qualify for any or all of these programs at different times in your lives.

To learn how the programs work and when and how to apply for benefits, call the U.S. Social Security Administration's toll free number, **1-800-772-1213**, between 7 a.m. and 7 p.m., Monday through Friday. A representative will explain programs, tell you about SSA publications and answer basic questions about benefits. You can also make appointments with your local Social Security office on this toll free line.

Recorded information and services are also available 24 hours a day on the same toll free line, but you'll need a touch-tone telephone. People who are hearing impaired may call the toll free TTY number any time of the day, Monday through Friday: **1-800-325-0778**.

The SSA also has a web site (http://www.ssa.gov) on which it posts information, some of it in both English and Spanish, about:

- Benefits
- How to request a personal estimate of what benefits you will be entitled to
- How to apply for benefits
- The location of all regional Social Security offices, including abroad
- How to report fraud
- Facts and figures about Social Security

- Laws and regulations governing benefits
- Policy governing Americans living abroad
- Important Supreme Court rulings
- Recent legislation affecting benefits
- Other resources and related web sites

The Social Security Administration even tested a way to allow you to request and receive directly online an estimate of the benefits for which you'll be eligible. It encountered problems that resulted in privacy violations because requested information was e-mailed to the wrong people. It discontinued the practice and at this writing you may request your estimate online or by mailing in a downloadable request form, but the actual estimate will be sent to you via regular mail. The SSA is currently working on correcting the technical problem and if corrected, it may reinstate the full online service. The best way to determine whether this has been done is to visit the web site.

Social Security Administration
Office of Public Inquiries
6401 Security Blvd.
Baltimore, MD 21235
Phone: 410-965-7700
Toll free: 800-772-1213
TTY: 800-325-0778
URL: http://www.ssa.gov/

MEDICARE

Medicare is a form of national health insurance that is designed primarily, but not exclusively, to benefit persons who are 65 and over. As with Social Security, Medicare was created by federal law, and the rules of coverage and eligibility apply equally throughout the country.

Its purpose is to help you pay your medical bills, not to pay all of your medical costs. Medicare pays for basic hospital care (Part A) and gives supplemental help with additional medical costs (Part B).

The hospitals, doctors and other health-care providers who treat Medicare recipients are not employed by the government. They are members of the private sector who have agreed to accept Medicare checks in partial payment for their services.

The Health Care Financing Administration (HCFA) coordinates the federal government's participation in Medicare. HCFA sponsors the Medicare Hotline, **1-800-638-6833**, which operates Monday through Friday, 8 a.m. to 8 p.m. It's an automated information line of recorded information about Medicare, as well as supplemental insurance such as Medigap, insurance policies that cover part or all of seniors' medical expenses that Medicare doesn't pay. You can also get Medicare information and applications at your local Social Security office.

HCFA has another important function: it collects and makes available information about—and investigates complaints against—Health Maintenance Organizations (HMOs) that receive Medicare or Medicaid payments. If you receive questionable care (or suspect fraud) from a federally-qualified HMO, you should contact HCFA through its toll free Medicare Hotline or write:

Health Care Financing Administration
P.O. Box 340
Columbia, MD 21045
Phone: 410-786-3000
Toll free: 800-638-6833 (Medicare Hotline)
Toll free: 800-655-1636 (Eligibility Requirements for Part A)
Toll free: 800-233-1124 (Eligibility Requirements for Part B)

MEDICAID

If you are over 65, you may also qualify for free medical assistance through Medicaid. The federal government created the program, but, unlike Medicare and Social Security, it is run by state governments. Thus, even though the rules of eligibility and coverage are governed by federal guidelines, within those guidelines the rules vary from state to state.

Persons over 65 and some disabled people may receive Medicaid payments. To be eligible, you must be considered financially needy. This is judged in one of two ways: either you have few financial assets (called "categorical" need), or your medical bills are high when compared to your assets ("medical" need). To qualify for payment:

- your expenses must be for services on a list approved for coverage by Medicaid;
- the care must have been prescribed by a doctor;
- it must be provided in a facility that accepts Medicaid;
- a Utilization Review Committee of the hospital or skilled nursing facility must determine that your inpatient care was "medically necessary."

Some services, such as elective surgery or dental work, require prior approval. Also, Medicaid will not pay bills that are covered by either Medicare or private insurance. You may be covered by both Medicare and private insurance and still qualify for Medicaid, but you may not collect twice for the same expense.

To learn more about Medicaid eligibility requirements and the types of services covered by Medicaid in your state, contact the **Health Care Financing Administration**   P.O. Box 340, Columbia, MD 21045, (410) 786-3000. Or, call the appropriate number below:

ALABAMA

800-362-1504	Information
800-253-0799	TDD
800-338-6046	Inpatient Review
800-204-3728	Non-Emergency Transportation (In-State)
800-545-1098	Healthy Beginnings
800-824-6584	Fraud Hotline
800-456-1242	Medicaid Automated Claims
800-252-8858	Blue Cross/Blue Shield
800-688-7989	EDS

ALASKA

907-561-2171	Medicaid/Information

ARIZONA

In-State only, except where noted

800-654-8713	General Information
800-523-0231	General Information (Out-of-State but not nationwide)
800-826-5140	TDD
800-962-6690	Verification Eligibility
800-334-5283	Enrollment/Plan
800-953-3227	Enrollment/Plan
800-405-7055	Emergency Services
800-342-0567	Long Term Care - Flagstaff
800-824-2656	Long Term Care - Tucson

ARKANSAS

800-482-5431	Medicaid Recipients
800-482-1141	Medicaid Providers
800-482-5850	Out-of-State callers and TDD ext. 22117

CALIFORNIA

800-952-5253	Medi-Cal Fair Hearings
800-722-0432	Medi-Cal Fraud and Patient Abuse
800-BABY-999	BABYCAL and AIM
800-322-6384	DENTICAL

Medi-Cal Managed Care

800-430-4362	English and languages not listed below
800-430-7077	TDD
800-430-5005	Cambodian
800-430-6006	Cantonese
800-430-2022	Hmong
800-430-4091	Lao
800-430-7007	Russian
800-430-3003	Spanish
800-430-8008	Vietnamese

COLORADO

800-221-3943	
800-659-3656	TDD

CONNECTICUT

800-445-5394	Dept. of Social Services
800-445-5394	Alternate Care
800-233-2503	CADAP Program
800-547-3443	CT Partnership LTC
800-385-4052	Electronic Benefit Transfer
800-443-9946	Elderly Services
800-842-1132	Energy Services
800-842-2155	Fraud Hotline
800-842-2159	General Assistance
800-609-5627	Jobs
800-445-5394	PASSAR
800-228-5437	Problem Resolution Unit
800-842-1508	Public Information
800-445-5394	Self-Directed Care
800-647-8872	Support Payment
800-842-4524	TDD
800-842-0012	Transportation

DELAWARE

In-State only

800-372-2022	General Information
800-924-3958	TDD
800-996-9969	Health Benefits Manager for Managed Care Enrollment

800-562-8080	SSI Recipients
800-435-5400	Long Term Care, Chronic Renal Disease Program & Institutional Services
800-642-4772	Long Term Care, Pre Admission Screening
800-336-3080	Long Term Care, Financial Eligibility

DISTRICT OF COLUMBIA

202-727-0735	Information
202-783-2118	Managed Care Helpline
202-279-6003	TDD

FLORIDA

In-State only

800-303-2422	Pensacola
800-699-7068	Panama City
800-248-2243	Tallahassee
800-803-3245	Ocala
800-940-4803	Flagler/Volusia
800-273-5880	Jacksonville
800-299-4844	Pasco County
800-606-1030	Brevard and Osceola
800-310-2473	Lee County
800-290-1447	West Palm Beach

GEORGIA

800-246-2757	Georgia Better Health Care
800-282-4536	Client Inquiry
800-656-8739	Client Appeals
800-533-0686	Fraud Control Line
800-766-4456	Provider Enrollment
800-869-1150	Welfare Information
800-934-9206	EPSDT/Health Check

HAWAII

Islands only

800-518-8887	Medicaid providers claims only
587-3521	Oahu (Applicants)
587-3540	Oahu (Recipients)
933-4112	Hawaii (East)
329-3454	Hawaii (West)
243-5750	Maui
241-3575	Kauai
800-553-3295	Molokai (Toll free calls to Maui)
800-894-5755	Lanai (Toll free calls to Maui)

IDAHO

In-State only

800-926-2588

ILLINOIS

800-252-8635	Medicaid Information
800-526-5812	TDD/Information
217-782-0963	Medicaid Information
800-226-0768	Managed Care Information
217-785-8036	Managed Care Information (Out-of-State calls)
800-842-1461	Provider Health Care Hotline
800-252-8903	Welfare & Medical Fraud
217-524-2596	Welfare & Medical Fraud (Out-of-State calls)
800-642-7588	Prescription Drug Prior Approval for providers (In-& Out-of-State)
217-782-5565	Pharmacy Coverage

INDIANA

800-433-0746	Family Help Line
800-545-7763	Disability, Aging & Rehabilitation Services
800-622-4968	Disability Determination
800-382-1039	Medicaid Provider Fraud
800-446-1993	Medicaid Recipient Fraud
800-992-4584	Child Support (In-State)
800-622-4932	Family Independence Policy (Nationwide)
800-992-6978	Adult Protective Service
800-889-9949	Hoosier Healthwise

In-State only

800-457-4518 Prior Authorization
800-577-1278 Provider Assistance
800-457-4584 Recipient Inquiries
800-457-4515 Surveillance and
              Utilization (SUR)
800-457-4510 Third Party Liability
              (TPL)

IOWA

In-State calls

800-532-1215 Recipients' Hotline
800-326-4132 Provider Hotline for
              Managed Care

KANSAS

800-766-9012 Recipients' Assistance Unit
800-933-6593 Provider Assistance Unit

KENTUCKY

In-State Only

800-752-6200 Child and Adult Abuse
800-432-9251 Crisis Line for Parents
800-432-9337 Drug and Alcohol
              Information
800-432-9346 Special Needs Adoption

In- and Out- of State

800-635-2570 KENPAC
800-232-KIDS Foster Care
800-372-2973 Ombudsman
800-372-2991 Nursing Home
              Ombudsman
800-372-2970 Welfare Fraud

LOUISIANA

800-327-3419 Home Health
              Complaints
800-488-2917 Fraud Reporting
504-342-3891 State Medicaid Agency

MAINE

In-State only

800-321-5557

MARYLAND

In-State only

800-284-4510 HMO Hotline
800-766-8692 Managed Care
800-685-5861 Medical Care Policy
800-456-8900 Pregnant Women and
              Children/Prenatal
              Assistance
800-445-1159 Medical Assistance
              Provider Relations
800-492-2134 Eligibility Verification
              System (EVS) for
              Providers
800-934-6704 Maryland Access to Care
800-445-1192 Provider Billing
              Questions
800-492-5231 Beneficiary Billing
              Questions
800-638-6252 AIDS General Information
              for Beneficiaries

MASSACHUSETTS

In-State only

800-842-2900 English & Spanish
800-469-6140 TDD

MICHIGAN

800-642-3195 General Information
800-292-2550 Provider Medical
              Assistance Information

MINNESOTA

800-657-3739 Health Care Programs
800-657-3672 Minnesota Care
800-366-8930 TTY

MISSISSIPPI

800-421-2408 Medicaid Information

MISSOURI

In-State only

800-392-2161 Recipient Services
800-392-0938 Provider Communications
800-392-8030 Pharmacy/Exceptions

MONTANA

In-State only

800-332-2272
800-833-8503 TTY

NEBRASKA

800-642-6092 Medicaid Eligibility
800-600-1297 Managed Care Helpline
800-332-0265 Claim Payment
800-569-0866 NHC
800-641-1902 Share Advantage
800-775-2752 The Wellness Option
800-710-8978 The Wellness Option
800-843-2374 HMO Nebraska, BC/BS
800-804-5022 Mental Health/Substance
              Abuse

In-State District Offices

800-843-1407 Alliance
800-554-9123 Beatrice
800-361-0039 Bridgeport
800-497-1515 Broken Bow
800-559-9718 Chadron
800-330-0755 Columbus
800-576-5212 David City
800-467-9922 Fremont
800-779-4855 Kearney
800-778-1613 Lexington
800-778-1612 McCook
800-884-6411 Nebraska City
800-782-8844 Norfolk
800-778-1611 North Platte
800-778-1614 Ogalala

800-776-1188 Plattsmouth
800-643-7415 Sidney
800-755-1333 Wahoo
800-557-8511 Wilber
800-627-3411 York

Nebraska Department of Social Services

800-652-1999 Adult/Child Abuse
800-831-4573 Child Support Hotline
800-358-8802 Disabled Persons &
              Family Support
800-358-8802 Medically Handicapped
              Children's Program
800-772-7368 Foster Parent Recruitment
800-272-5900 Foster Parent Training
800-833-7352 TDD/TTY Users
800-833-0920 Voice Users

NEVADA

In-State only

800-992-0900

NEW HAMPSHIRE

In-State only

800-852-3345
800-735-2964 TDD

NEW JERSEY

800-776-6334 General Information
800-701-0710 Medicaid Managed Care

NEW MEXICO

New Mexico and Arizona callers

800-432-6217 English and Spanish
800-926-4296 Primary Care Network
888-997-2583 Medicaid Managed Care
800-609-4833 TDD

NEW YORK

800-428-9097 Beneficiaries & Providers
800-541-2831 Only for Medicaid/
              Pharmaceutical Co -
              Payment Issues

NORTH CAROLINA

In-State only

800-662-7030 CARE-LINE

NORTH DAKOTA

In-State only

800-755-2604 English & Spanish

OHIO

800-590-9864 Medical Operations
800-686-1548 Rx-Prior Authorization
800-686-6108 Home & Community
              Based Services
800-686-6108 Long-Term Care
800-627-8133 Fraud Control/Welfare
800-755-4769 Prenatal Wellchild/
              Help Me Grow
800-324-8680 Medicaid Hotline
800-686-1516 Provider Relations
800-686-1595 Food Stamps

OKLAHOMA

In-State only

800-522-0310 Customer Services
800-522-0114 Pharmacy Providers
800-871-9347 Provider Enrollment
800-767-3949 Recipient Eligibility
              Verification System
800-987-7767 SoonerCare
800-268-5261 Third Party Liability

OREGON

800-527-5772 Medicaid Information
800-282-8096 Aged & Disabled
800-359-9517 Oregon Health Plan
              Application
800-273-0557 Oregon Health Plan
              Client Hotline
800-365-8135 Oregon Health Plan
              Ombudsman Office

PENNSYLVANIA

717-787-1870 SMA number

RHODE ISLAND

In-State only

800-346-1004 Rite Care Information
800-299-8444 Spanish Information
800-745-5555 TDD

Toll Free Calls to Medicaid District Offices

800-675-9397 Newport
800-862-0222 North Kingstown
800-984-8989 Pawtucket
800-471-1757 Warwick

SOUTH CAROLINA

800-834-1640 Medicaid Eligibility
800-544-0820 Managed Care
              Enrollment
800-763-9087 Appeals & Hearings

SOUTH DAKOTA

605-773-3495 SMA number

TENNESSEE

800-669-1851 Medicaid Tenncare
              Information (English)
800-254-7568 Medicaid Tenncare
              Information (Spanish)

TEXAS

In- & Out-of-State

800-252-8263 TDH/Medicaid
800-964-2777 STAR Health Plan
800-436-6184 Fraud Abuse Hotline
800-792-1109 Rehabilitation Services
800-252-8010 Hospice Hotline
800-228-4901 Utilization & Assess-
              ment Review

In-State only

800-844-8894 Client Eligibility Inquiry
800-223-8358 QUEST
800-456-9858 Information Services for
              Long Term Care Facilities
800-252-8016 Consumer Services for
              Nursing Facility Residents
800-458-9858 Long Term Care
              Complaint Line

UTAH

800-662-9651 (For UT, CO, WY, AZ,
              NV, and ID only;
              Spanish interpreters
              available.)

VERMONT

In-State only

800-987-2839

VIRGINIA

800-552-8627 Medicaid Provider
800-358-5050 Transportation Helpline
800-643-2273 Medallion/HMO
800-421-7376 Maternal & Child Health
800-884-9730 Eligibility Helpline

WASHINGTON

800-562-3022 Medical Assistance
              Customer Service
              Center(Nationwide)
800-848-5429 TTY
800-562-6906 Fraud Hotline

WEST VIRGINIA

800-688-5810 Medicaid Eligibility
800-642-3607 Provider Services -
              Billing
800-926-1700 Medical Assistance
800-633-4340 Consumer Claims
800-433-3019 Provider Relations

WISCONSIN

800-362-3002

WYOMING

800-251-1268
307-777-5648 TDD

STATE OFFICES ON AGING

The State Agencies on Aging can act on your behalf to help you resolve problems with governmental or private institutions. For example, they can contact the Social Security office on your behalf to get answers to questions you have about monthly checks, benefits or rights. Or, they could investigate complaints against a nursing home or local business. They can also provide legal advice and referrals but they cannot provide legal representation to individuals. If the agency can't resolve your problem directly, they'll usually find someone or an agency that can.

ALABAMA

Martha Murph Beck, Ex. Director
Alabama Commission on Aging
RSA Plaza, Ste. 470
770 Washington Ave.
Montgomery, AL 36130
Phone: 334-242-5743
Fax: 334-242-5594
TDD: 334-242-0995

ALASKA

Jane Demmert, Director
Alaska Commission on Aging
Division of Senior Services
P.O. Box 110211
Juneau, AK 99811-0211
Phone: 907-465-3250
Fax: 907-465-4716

ARIZONA

Aging and Adult Administration
Site Code 950A
Department of Economic Security
1789 W. Jefferson St.
Phoenix, AZ 85007
Phone: 602-542-4446
Fax: 602-542-6575

ARKANSAS

Herb Sanderson, Director
Division of Aging and Adult Services
Department of Human Services
P.O. Box 1437, Slot 1412
Little Rock, AR 72203-1437
Phone: 501-682-2441
Fax: 501-682-8155

CALIFORNIA

Dixon Arnett, Director
Department of Aging
1600 K St.
Sacramento, CA 95814
Phone: 916-322-3887
Fax: 916-324-1903
TDD toll free: 800-735-2929

COLORADO

Rita Barreras, Director
Aging and Adult Service
Department of Social Services
110 16th St., Ste. 200
Denver, CO 80202-4147
Voice/TDD: 303-620-4147
Fax: 303-620-4191

CONNECTICUT

Christine M. Lewis
Director, Community Services
Department of Social Services
Elderly Services Division
25 Sigourney St., 10th Fl.
Hartford, CT 06106-5033
Phone: 860-424-5277
Toll free in CT: 800-842-1508
Fax: 860-424-4966

DELAWARE

Eleanor L. Cain, Director
Div. Services for Aging and Adults
 with Physical Disabilities, DDHSS
1901 N. DuPont Hwy.
New Castle, DE 19720
Phone: 302-577-4791
Toll free: 800-223-9074
Fax: 301-577-4793

DISTRICT OF COLUMBIA

Jearline F. Williams, Ex. Director
D.C. Office on Aging
441 4th St., NW, Ste. 900 South
Washington, DC 20001
Phone: 202-724-5622
Fax: 202-724-4979
TDD: 202-724-8925

FLORIDA

Bentley Lipscomb, Secretary
Florida Department of Elder Affairs
4040 Esplanade Way
Tallahassee, FL 32399-7000
Phone: 904-414-2000
Fax: 904-414-2004
TDD: 904-414-2001

GEORGIA

Judy Hagebak, Director
Division of Aging Services
Department of Human Resources
2 Peachtree St., NE, 18th Fl.
Atlanta, GA 30303
Phone: 404-657-5258
Fax: 404-657-5285

HAWAII

Marilyn Seely, Director
Executive Office on Aging
250 S. Hotel St., Ste. 107
Honolulu, HI 96813-2831
Phone: 808-586-0100
Toll free in HI: 800-468-4644
Fax: 808-586-0185

IDAHO

Arlene D. Davidson, Director
Idaho Commission on Aging
700 W. Jefferson, Rm. 108
P.O. Box 83720
Boise, ID 83720-0007
Phone: 208-334-3833
Fax: 208-334-3033

ILLINOIS

Maralee Lindley, Director
Department on Aging
421 E. Capitol Ave., Ste. 100
Springfield, IL 62701-1789
Phone: 217-785-2870
Voice/TDD in IL: 800-252-8966
Fax: 217-785-4477
Chicago Office: 312-814-2630

INDIANA

Bobby Conner, Director
Division of Disability, Aging
and Rehabilitative Service
Bureau of Aging and In-Home Services
402 W. Washington St.
Indianapolis, IN 46207-7083
Phone: 317-232-1147
Voice/TDD in IN: 800-962-8408
Toll free: 800-545-7763
Fax: 317-232-7867

IOWA

Betty Grandquist, Ex. Director
Department of Elder Affairs
Clemens Bldg., 3rd Fl.
200 Tenth St.
Des Moines, IA 50309-3609
Phone: 515-281-5187
Fax: 515-281-4036
TDD: 515-281-5188

KANSAS

Thelma Hunter Gordon, Secretary
Department on Aging
Docking State Office Bldg., Rm. 150
915 S.W. Harrison
Topeka, KS 66612-1505
Phone: 913-296-4986
Toll free in KS: 800-432-3535
TDD: 913-291-3167

KENTUCKY

Department of Social Services
CHR Bldg. - 5th West
275 E. Main St.
Frankfort, KY 40621
Phone: 502-564-6930
Fax: 502-564-4595

LOUISIANA

Richard W. Collins
Governor's Office of Elderly Affairs
P.O. Box 80374
Baton Rouge, LA 70898-0374
Phone: 504-925-1700
Toll free in LA: 800-259-4990
Fax: 504-925-1749

MAINE

Christine Gianopoulos, Director
Bureau of Elder and Adult Services
Department of Human Services
35 Anthony Ave.
State House, Station 11
Augusta, ME 04333-0011
Phone: 207-624-5335
Fax: 207-624-5361

MARYLAND

Sue Fryer Ward, Director
Office on Aging
State Office Bldg., Rm. 1004
301 W. Preston St.
Baltimore, MD 21201
Phone: 410-767-1102
Toll free in MD: 800-243-3425
Fax: 410-333-7943
TDD: 410-767-1083

MASSACHUSETTS

Franklin P. Ollivierre, Secretary
Executive Office of Elder Affairs
One Ashburton Pl., 5th Fl.
Boston, MA 02108
Phone: 617-727-7750
Toll free in MA: 800-882-2003
Fax: 617-727-9368
TDD Toll free: 800-872-0166

MICHIGAN

Carol Parr, Acting Director
Office of Services to the Aging
P.O. Box 30026
Lansing, MI 48909
Phone: 517-373-8230
Fax: 517-373-4092
TDD: 517-373-4096

MINNESOTA

James G. Varpness, Ex. Secretary
Minnesota Board on Aging
444 Lafayette Rd.
St. Paul, MN 55155-3843
Phone: 612-296-2770
Toll free: 800-882-6262
Fax: 612-297-7855

MISSISSIPPI

Eddie Anderson, Director
Division of Aging and
Adult Services
750 N. State St.
Jackson, MS 39202
Phone: 601-359-4925
Toll free in MS: 800-948-3090
Fax: 601-359-4370

MISSOURI

Greg Vadner, Director
Division on Aging
Department of Social Services
P.O. Box 1337
615 Howerton Ct.
Jefferson City, MO 65102-1337
Phone: 573-751-3082
Fax: 573-751-8687
TDD Toll free: 800-735-2966

MONTANA

Charles Rehbein
Bureau Chief
Office on Aging
111 N. Sanders, Rm. 210
Helena, MT 59620
Phone: 406-444-4077
Toll free: 800-332-2272
TDD Toll free: 800-833-8503
Fax: 406-444-7433

NEBRASKA

Dennis H. Loose, Director
Department on Aging
P.O. Box 95044
301 Centennial Mall-South
Lincoln, NE 68509-5044
Phone: 402-471-2306
Voice/TDD in NE: 800-942-7830
Fax: 402-471-4619

NEVADA

Mary Liveratti
Acting Administrator
Division for Aging Services
Department of Human Resources
340 N. 11th St., Ste. 203
Las Vegas, NV 89101
Phone: 702-486-3545
Fax: 702-486-3572
TDD: 702-486-3420

NEW HAMPSHIRE

Thomas E. Pryor, Director
Division of Elderly and
Adult Services
State Office Park South
115 Pleasant St., Annex Bldg. #1
Concord, NH 03301-6501
Phone: 603-271-4680
Toll free in NH: 800-351-1888
Fax: 603-271-4643
TDD Toll free in NH: 800-735-2964

NEW JERSEY

Ruth Reader
Assistant Commissioner
Department of Health and
Senior Services
Division of Senior Affairs
101 S. Broad St., #CN 807
Trenton, NJ 08625-0807
Phone: 609-292-3766
Toll free in NJ: 800-792-8820
Fax: 609-633-6609

NEW MEXICO

Michelle Lujan Grishan, Director
State Agency on Aging
La Villa Rivera Building
228 E. Palace Ave., Ground Fl.
Santa Fe, NM 87501
Phone: 505-827-7640
Toll free in NM: 800-432-2080
Fax: 505-827-7649

NEW YORK

Walter G. Hoefer, Director
New York State Office
for the Aging
2 Empire State Plaza
Albany, NY 12223-1251
Phone: 518-474-5731
Voice/TDD in NY: 800-342-9871
Fax: 518-474-0608

NORTH CAROLINA

Bonnie Cramer, Director
Division of Aging
CB 29531
693 Palmer Dr.
Raleigh, NC 27626-0531
Phone: 919-733-3983
Fax: 919-733-0443

NORTH DAKOTA

Linda Wright, Director
Department of Human Services
600 S. 2nd St., Ste. 1C
Bismarck, ND 58507-5729
Phone: 701-328-8910
Toll free in ND: 800-755-8521
Fax: 701-328-8989

OHIO

Judith V. Brachman, Director
Ohio Department of Aging
50 W. Broad St., 9th Fl.
Columbus, OH 43215-5928
Phone: 614-466-5500
Fax: 614-466-5741

OKLAHOMA

Roy R. Keen
Division Administrator
Services for the Aging
Department of Human Services
P.O. Box 25352
Oklahoma City, OK 73125
Phone: 405-521-2281; 521-2327
Toll free in OK: 800-211-2116
Fax: 405-521-2086

OREGON

Roger Averback, Administrator
Senior and Disabled
Services Division
500 Summer St., NE, 2nd Fl.
Salem, OR 97310-1015
Voice/TDD: 503-945-5811
Toll free in OR: 800-282-8096
Fax: 503-373-7823

PENNSYLVANIA

Richard Browdie, Secretary
Department of Aging
400 Market St., 6th Fl.
Harrisburg, PA 17101-2301
Phone: 717-783-1550
Fax: 717-772-3382

PUERTO RICO

Ruby Rodriguez Ramirez
M.H.S.A Executive Director
Governor's Office of Elderly Affairs
Call Box 50063
Old San Juan Station, PR 00902
Phone: 787-721-5710
Fax: 787-721-6510

RHODE ISLAND

Barbara Casey Ruffino, Director
Department of Elderly Affairs
160 Pine St.
Providence, RI 02903-3708
Phone: 401-277-2858
TDD toll free in RI: 800-322-2880
Fax: 401-277-1490
TDD: 401-277-2880

SOUTH CAROLINA

Constance C. Rinehart, Ex. Director
South Carolina Division on Aging
202 Arbor Lake Dr., Ste. 301
Columbia, SC 29223-4535
Phone: 803-737-7500
Toll free in SC: 800-868-9095
Fax: 803-737-7501

SOUTH DAKOTA

Gail Ferris, Administrator
Office of Adult Services and Aging
Richard Kneip Building
700 Governors Dr.
Pierre, SD 57501-2291
Phone: 605-773-3656
Fax: 605-773-6834

TENNESSEE

Emily Wiseman, Director
Commission on Aging
500 Deaderick St.
Andrew Jackson Bldg., 9th Fl.
Nashville, TN 37243-0860
Phone: 615-741-2056
Fax: 615-741-3309
TDD toll free: 800-848-0298
Voice relay service: 800-848-0299

TEXAS

Mary Sapp, Ex. Director
Department on Aging
4900 N. Lamar
Austin, TX 78751-2399
Phone: 512-424-6840
Toll free: 800-252-9240
Fax: 512-424-6890

UTAH

Helen Goddard, Director
Division of Aging and
Adult Services
P.O. Box 45500
120 N. 200 West, Ste. 401
Salt Lake City, UT 84145-0500
Phone: 801-538-3910
Fax: 801-538-4395

VERMONT

David Yacozone, Commissioner
Department of Aging and Disabilities
Waterbury Complex
103 S. Main St.
Waterbury, VT 05676
Voice/TDD: 802-241-2400
Fax: 802-241-2325

VIRGIN ISLANDS

Catherine L. Mills, Commissioner
Department of Human Services
Knud Hansen Complex, Bldg. A
1303 Hospital Ground
Charlotte Amalie, VI 00802
Phone: 809-774-0930
Fax: 809-774-3466

VIRGINIA

Thelma Bland, Commissioner
Department for the Aging
700 E. Franklin St., 10th Fl.
Richmond, VA 23219-2327
Voice/TDD: 804-225-2271
Toll free in VA: 800-552-3402
Fax: 804-371-8381

WASHINGTON

Ralph Smith, Asst, Secretary
Aging and Adult Services
Dept. of Social and Health Services
P.O. Box 45600
Olympia, WA 98504-5600
Phone: 360-493-2500
Toll free: 800-422-3263
Fax: 360-493-9484
TDD: 360-493-2637

WEST VIRGINIA

William E. Lytton, Jr.
Interim Executive Director
Commission on Aging
1900 Kanawha Blvd., East
Holly Grove-Bldg. 10
Charleston, WV 25305-0160
Phone: 304-558-3317
Fax: 304-558-0004

WISCONSIN

Donna McDowell, Director
Bureau on Aging
Dept. of Health and Family Services
217 S. Hampton St., Ste. 300
Madison, WI 53703
Phone: 608-266-2536
Fax: 608-267-3203

WYOMING

Deborah Fleming, Administrator
Department of Health
Division on Aging
139 Hathaway Bldg., Rm. 139
Cheyenne, WY 82002-0480
Phone: 307-777-7986
Toll free: 800-442-2766
Fax: 307-777-5340

LONG-TERM CARE OMBUDSMAN

If you are having problems with the care you or a loved one is receiving in a nursing home or other long-term care facility— and you haven't had any luck resolving the problem on your own —you should contact your state's Long-Term Care Ombudsman program.

Ombudsmen investigate and resolve complaints made by or on behalf of residents of nursing homes, boards and care homes, and similar adult homes. They are well-trained and are generally committed to resolving disputes that arise under their jurisdiction. Many promote policies and practices to improve the quality of life, health, safety, and rights of long-term care residents.

For information regarding care of older persons in long-term care facilties, call your state's office, listed below.

ALASKA

Frances Purdy
State LTC Ombudsman
Older Alaskans Commission
State LTC Ombudsman Office
3601 C St., Ste. 260
Anchorage, AK 99503-5209
Phone: 907-563-6393
Fax: 907-561-3862

ALABAMA

Marie Tomlin
State LTC Ombudsman
Commission on Aging
770 Washington Ave.
RSA Plaza, Ste. 470
Montgomery, AL 36130
Phone: 334-242-5743
Fax: 334-242-5594

ARKANSAS

Raymon Harvey
State LTC Ombudsman
Division of Aging & Adult Services
State LTC Ombudsman Office
Office P.O. Box 1437
Donaghey Plaza, South, Slot 1412
Little Rock, AR 72203-1437
Phone: 501-682-2441
Fax: 501-682-8155

ARIZONA

Rosalind Webster
State LTC Ombudsman
Aging & Adult Adminstration
1789 W. Jefferson 950A
Phoenix, AZ 85007
Phone: 602-542-4446
Fax: 602-542-6575

CALIFORNIA

Phyllis Heath
State LTC Ombudsman
California Dept. of Aging
1600 K St.
Sacramento, CA 95814
Phone: 916-323-6681
Fax: 916-323-7299

COLORADO

Virginia Fraser
State LTC Ombudsman
The Legal Center
455 Sherman St., Ste. 130
Denver, CO 80203
Phone: 303-722-0300
Fax: 303-722-0720

CONNECTICUT

Barbara Frank
State LTC Ombudsman
CT Dept. on Aging
Dept. of Social Services
25 Sigourney St., 10th Fl.
Hartford, CT 06106-5033
Phone: 860-424-5200
Fax: 860-424-4966

DELAWARE

Maxine Nichols
State LTC Ombudsman
DH&SS Division
Services for the Aging & Disabled
New Castle County
256 Chapman Rd., Oxford Bldg., Ste. 200
Newark, DE 19702
Phone: 302-453-3820
Fax: 302-453-3836

DISTRICT OF COLUMBIA

Deidre Rye/Anne Hart
State LTC Ombudsman
AARP-Legal Counsel for the Elderly
State LTC Ombudsman Office
601 E St., NW, 4th Fl., Bldg. A
Washington, DC 20049
Phone: 202-662-4933
Fax: 202-434-6464

FLORIDA

Gwen Schaper
State LTC Ombudsman
State LTC Ombudsman Council
Carlton Bldg., Office of the Governor
501 S. Calhoun St.
Tallahassee, Fl 32399-0001
Phone: 904-488-6190
Fax: 904-488-5657

GEORGIA

Becky Kurtz
LTC State Ombudsman
Division of Aging Services
2 Peachtree St., NW, 18th Fl.
Atlanta, GA 30303 -3176
Phone: 404-657-5319
Fax: 404-657-5285

HAWAII

Michael Ragsdale
State LTC Ombudsman
Office of the Governor
Executive Office on Aging
250 S. Hotel St., Ste. 107
Honolulu, HI 96813-2831
Phone: 808-586-0100
Fax: 808-586-0185

IDAHO

Cathy Hart
State LTC Ombudsman
Idaho Office on Aging
P.O. Box 83720
Statehouse, Rm. 108
Boise, ID 83720-0007
Phone: 208-334-3822
Fax: 208-334-3033

ILLINOIS

Beverly Rowley / Nyena Johnson
State LTC Ombudsmen
Illinois Dept. on Aging
421 E. Capitol Ave., Ste. 100
Springfield, IL 62701-1789
Phone: 217-785-3143
Fax: 217-785-4477

INDIANA

Robyn Grant
State LTC Ombudsman
Division of Aging & Rehab Services
P.O. Box 708 3-W454
402 W. Washington St., #W-454
Indianapolis, IN 46207-7083
Phone: 317-232-7134
Fax: 317-232-7867

IOWA

Carl M. McPherson
State LTC Ombudsman
Iowa Dept. of Elder Affairs
Clemens Bldg.
200 10th St., 3rd Fl.
Des Moines, IA 50309-3609
Phone: 515-281-4656
Fax: 515-281-4036

KANSAS

Myron Dunavan
State LTC Ombudsman
Kansas Dept. on Aging
915 S.W. Harrison-docking, #122 S
Topeka, KS 66612-1500
Phone: 913-296-6539
Fax: 913-296-0256

KENTUCKY

Gary R. Hammonds
State LTC Ombudsman
Division of Aging Services
State LTC Ombudsman Office
275 E. Main St., 5th Fl., W
Frankfort, KY 40621
Phone: 502-564-6930
Fax: 502-564-4595

LOUISIANA

Linda Sadden
State LTC Ombudsman
Governor's Office of Elderly Affairs
State LTC Ombudsman Office
4550 North Blvd., 2nd Fl.
Baton Rouge, LA 70806
Phone: 504-342-7100
Fax: 504-342-7133

MAINE

Brenda Gallant
State LTC Ombudsman
State LTC Ombudsman Program
21 Bangor St.
P.O. Box 126
Augusta, ME 04332-0126
Toll free: 800-499-0229 (In-State only)
Phone: 207-621-1079
Fax: 207-621-0509

MARYLAND

Patricia Bayliss
State LTC Ombudsman
Maryland Office on Aging
301 W. Preston St., Rm. 1004
Baltimore, MD 21201
Phone: 410-225-1074
Fax: 410-333-7943

MASSACHUSETTS

Mary Mckenna
State LTC Ombudsman
Exec. Office of Elder Affairs
1 Ashburton Pl., 5th Fl.
Boston, MA 02108-1518
Phone: 617-727-7750
Fax: 617-727-9368

MICHIGAN

Hollis Turnham
State LTC Ombudsman
Citizens for Better Care
State LTC Ombudsman Office
416 N. Homer St., Ste. 101
Lansing, MI 48912-4700
Phone: 517-336-6753
Fax: 517-336-7718

MINNESOTA

Sharon Zoesch
State LTC Ombudsman
Office of Ombudsman
444 Lafayette Rd., 4th Fl.
St. Paul, MN 55155-3843
Phone: 612-296-0382
Fax: 612-297-7855

MISSISSIPPI

Anniece Mclemore
State LTC Ombudsman
Division of Aging & Adult Services
750 N. State St.
Jackson, MS 39202
Phone: 601-359-4929
Fax: 601-359-4970

MISSOURI

Carol Scott
State LTC Ombudsman
Missouri Division of Aging
Dept. Social Services
P.0. Box 1337
Jefferson City, MO 65102-1337
Phone: 573-526-0727
Fax: 573-751-8687

MONTANA

Doug Blakley
State LTC Ombudsman
Senior and Long Term Care Division
Dept. of Public Health & Human Services
P.O. Box 8005
Helena, MT 59604-8005
Phone: 406-444-5900
Fax: 406-444-7743

NEBRASKA

Geri Tucker
State LTC Ombudsman
NE Dept. on Aging
301 Centennial Mall South
P.O. Box 95044
Lincoln, NE 68509-5044
Phone: 402-471-2306
Fax: 402-471-4619

NEVADA

Bruce McAnnany
State LTC Ombudsman
Compliance Investigator
Dept. of Human Resources
340 N. 11th St., Ste. 203
Las Vegas, NV 89101
Phone: 702-486-3545
Fax: 702-486-3572

NEW HAMPSHIRE

Judith Griffin
Acting State LTC Ombudsman
Division of Elderly & Adult Services
State LTC Ombudsman Office
6 Hazen Dr.
Concord, NH 03301-6505
Phone: 603-271-4375
Toll free: 800-443-5640 (In-State only)
Fax: 603-271-4643

NEW JERSEY

Bonnie Kelly
State LTC Ombudsman
Ombudsman Office For
Institutionalized Elderly
101 S. Broad St., 6th Fl.
Trenton, NJ 08625-0808
Phone: 609-984-7831
Fax: 609-984-8153

NEW MEXICO

Tim Covell
State LTC Ombudsman
State Agency on Aging
State LTC Ombudsman Office
228 E. Palace Ave., Ste. A
Santa Fe, NM 87501
Phone: 505-827-7663
Fax: 505-827-7649

NEW YORK

Faith Fish
State LTC Ombudsman
NYS Office for the Aging
2 Empire State Plaza
Albany, NY 12223-0001
Phone: 518-474-0108
Fax: 518-474-0608

NORTH CAROLINA

Michael McCann
State LTC Ombudsman
Division of Aging
693 Palmer Dr.
Caller Box Number 29531
Raleigh, NC 27626-0531
Phone: 919-733-3983
Fax: 919-733-0443

NORTH DAKOTA

Jo Hildebrant
State LTC Ombudsman
Dept. of Human Services
Aging Services Division
600 S. 2nd St., Ste. 1C
Bismarck, ND 58504
Phone: 701-328-2577
Fax: 701-221-5466

OHIO

Beverley Laubert
State LTC Ombudsman
Ohio Dept. of Aging
50 W. Broad St., 9th Fl.
Columbus, OH 43215-5928
Phone: 614-466-7922
Fax: 614-466-5741

OKLAHOMA

Esther Houser
State LTC Ombudsman
Aging Services Division
OK Department of Human Services
312 N.E. 28 St.
Oklahoma City, OK 73105
Phone: 405-521-6734
Fax: 405-521-2086

OREGON

Meredith A. Cote
State LTC Ombudsman
Office of the LTC Ombudsman
3855 Wolverine NE, Ste. 6
Salem, OR 97310
Phone: 503-378-6533
Fax: 503-373-0852

PENNSYLVANIA

Joyce O'Brien
State LTC Ombudsman
PA Dept. of Aging
LTC Ombudsman Program
400 Market St., 6th Fl.
Harrisburg, PA 17101-2301
Phone: 717-783-7247
Fax: 717-783-6842

PUERTO RICO

Norma Venegas
State LTC Ombudsman
Governor's Office of Elderly Affairs
Call Box 50063
Old San Juan Station
San Juan, PR 00902
Phone: 809-721-8225
Fax: 809-721-6510

RHODE ISLAND

Denise Medeiros
State LTC Ombudsman
Dept. of Elderly Affairs
160 Pine St.
Providence, RI 02903-3708
Phone: 401-277-2858
Fax: 401-277-2130

SOUTH CAROLINA

Mary B. Fagan
State LTC Ombudsman
Division on Aging
202 Arbor Lake Dr., Ste. 301
Columbia, SC 29223-4535
Phone: 803-737-7500
Fax: 803-737-7501

SOUTH DAKOTA

Jeff Askew
State LTC Ombudsman
Office of Adult Services & Aging
Dept. of Social Services
700 Governors Dr.
Pierre, SD 57501-2291
Phone: 605-773-3656
Fax: 605-773-6834

TENNESSEE

Adrian Wheeler
State LTC Ombudsman
Tennessee Commission on Aging
Andrew Jackson Bldg., 9th Fl.
500 Deaderick St.
Nashville, TN 37243-0860
Phone: 615-741-2056
Fax: 615-741-3309

TEXAS

John F. Willis
State LTC Ombudsman
Texas Dept. on Aging
State LTC Ombudsman Office
4900 N. Lamar Blvd.
Austin, TX 78751-2316
Phone: 512-444-2727
Fax: 512-440-5252

UTAH

Carol Bloswick
State LTC Ombudsman
Dept of Human Services
Div. of Aging & Adult Svcs
120 N. 200 West, Rm. 401
Salt Lake City, UT 84103
Phone: 801-538-3910
Fax: 801-538-4395

VERMONT

Jacqueline Majoros
State LTC Ombudsman
Vermont Legal Aid, Inc.
264 N. Winooski
P.O. Box 1367
Burlington, VT 05402
Phone: 802-863-5620
Fax: 802-863-7152

VIRGINIA

Mark Miller
State LTC Ombudsman Program
VA Association of Area
Agencies on Aging
530 E. Main St., Ste. 428
Richmond, VA 23219-2327
Phone: 804-644-2923
Fax: 804-644-5640

WASHINGTON

Kary W. Hyre
State LTC Ombudsman
So. King County Multi-Service Center
State LTC Ombudsman Office
1200 S. 336th St.
Federal Way, WA 98003-7452
Phone: 206-838-6810
Fax: 206-874-7831

WEST VIRGINIA

Carolyn S. Riffle
DHHR Specialist
WV Commission on Aging
State LTC Ombudsman Office
1900 Kanawha Blvd., East
Charleston, WV 25305-0160
Phone: 304-558-3317
Fax: 304-558-0004

WISCONSIN

George F. Potaracke
State LTC Ombudsman
Board on Aging & Long Term Care
214 N. Hamilton St.
Madison, WI 53703-2118
Phone: 608-266-8944
Fax: 608-261-6570

WYOMING

Deborah Alden
State LTC Ombudsman
WY Senior Citizens Inc.
756 Gilchrist
P.O. Box 94
Wheatland, WY 82201
Phone: 307-322-5553
Fax: 307-322-2890

ORGANIZATIONS

The following state and national organizations provide free information on their topic areas. Many also provide services and/or referrals to local resources. The list below is excerpted, in part, from the *Resource Directory for Older People*, National Institute on Aging, March, 1996.

ALZHEIMER'S ASSOCIATION
919 N. Michigan Ave., Ste. 1000
Chicago, IL 60611
Phone: 312-335-8700
Toll free: 800-621-0379

AMERICAN ASSOCIATION OF RETIRED PERSONS
601 E St., NW
Washington, DC 20049
Phone: 202-434-2277

AMERICAN HEART ASSOCIATION
7272 Greenville Ave.
Dallas, TX 75231
Phone: 214-373-6300
Toll free: 800-553-6321 (stroke survivor information)

AMERICAN LUNG ASSOCIATION
1740 Broadway
New York, NY 10019-4374
Phone: 212-315-8700
Toll free: 800-586-4872

AMERICAN OSTEOPATHIC ASSOCIATION
142 E. Ontario St.
Chicago, IL 6-611
Phone: 312-280-5854
Toll free: 800-621-1773

AMERICAN PARKINSON'S DISEASE ASSOCIATION
1250 Hylan Blvd., Ste. 4B
Staten Island, NY 10305
Phone: 718-981-8001
Toll free: 800-223-2732

ARTHRITIS FOUNDATION
1314 Spring St., NW
Atlanta, GA 30309
Phone: 404-872-7100

BETTER HEARING INSTITUTE
P.O. Box 1840
Washington, DC 20013
Phone: 703-642-0580
Toll free: 800-327-9355

CALIFORNIA ADVOCATES FOR NURSING HOME REFORM (C.A.N.H.R.)
1610 Bush St.
San Francisco, CA 94109
Phone: 415-474-5171

CHILDREN OF AGING PARENTS
1609 Woodbourne Rd.
Levittown, PA 19057
Phone: 215-945-6900
Toll free: 800-227-7294

CHOICE IN DYING
200 Varick St.
New York, NY 10014
Phone: 212-366-5540 (information on living wills & health care directives)

DELTA SOCIETY
289 Perimeter Rd., East
Renton, WA 98055-1329
Phone: 206-226-7357
Toll free: 800-869-6898 (promotes animal-assisted therapy programs)

DEPARTMENT OF VETERANS AFFAIRS
Office of Public Affairs
810 Vermont Ave., NW
Washington, DC 20420
Phone: 202-273-5700
Toll free: 800-827-1000

DES ACTION
1615 Broadway, Ste. 510
Oakland, CA 94612
Phone: 510-465-4011
Toll free: 800-DES-9288 (information about the drug DES)

FUNERAL AND MEMORIAL SOCIETIES OF AMERICA
P.O. Box 10
Hinesburg, VT 05461
Phone: 802-482-3437 (information on choosing a meaningful, dignified, affordable funeral)

GRAY PANTHERS
2025 Pennsylvania Ave., NW, Ste. 821
Washington, DC 20006
Phone: 202-466-3132

HEALTH CARE FINANCING ADMINISTRATION
P.O. Box 340
Columbia, MD 21045
Phone: 410-786-3000
Toll free: 800-638-6833
(Medicare Hotline)

HILL-BURTON PROGRAM
Health Resources and Services Administration
5600 Fishers Ln., Rm. 11-31
Rockville, MD 20857
Phone: 301-443-5656
Toll free: 800-638-0742 (hospital care)
Toll free: 800-492-0359 (in Maryland)

INTERNATIONAL ANTI-EUTHANASIA TASK FORCE
P.O. Box 760
Steubenville, OH 43952
Phone: 614-282-3810

NATIONAL ASSOCIATION FOR HOME CARE
228 7th St., SE
Washington, DC 20003
Phone: 202-547-7424

NATIONAL CANCER INSTITUTE
Office of Cancer Communications
Bldg. 31, Rm. 10A07
31 Center Dr., MSC 2580
Bethesda, MD 20892-2580
Phone: 301-496-5583
Toll free: 800-422-6237

NATIONAL CITIZENS' COALITION FOR NURSING HOME REFORM
1424 16th St., NW, Ste. 202
Washington, DC 20036-2211
Phone: 202-332-2275

NATIONAL COMMITTEE TO PRESERVE SOCIAL SECURITY AND MEDICARE
2000 K St., NW, Ste. 800
Washington, DC 20006
Phone: 202-822-9459
Toll free: 800-988-0180

THE NATIONAL COUNCIL ON THE AGING
409 3rd St., SW, Ste. 200
Washington, DC 20024
Phone: 202-479-1200

NATIONAL HOSPICE ORGANIZATION
1901 N. Moore St., Ste. 901
Arlington, VA 22209
Phone: 703-243-5900
Toll free: 800-658-8898

NATIONAL INSTITUTE ON AGING
Public Information Office
Bldg. 31, Rm. 5C27
31 Center Dr., MSC 2292
Bethesda, MD 20892-2292
Phone: 301-496-1752
Toll free: 800-222-2225

THE NATIONAL SENIOR CITIZENS LAW CENTER
1815 H St., NW, Ste. 700
Washington, DC 20006
Phone: 202-887-5280

NATIONAL SLEEP FOUNDATION
1367 Connecticut Ave., NW, Ste. 200
Washington, DC 20036
Phone: 202-785-2300

THE OLDER WOMEN'S LEAGUE
666 11th St., NW, Ste. 700
Washington, DC 20001
Phone: 202-783-6687
Toll free: 800-825-3695

PENSION RIGHTS CENTER
918 16th St., NW, Ste. 704
Washington, DC 20006
Phone: 202-296-3776

PEOPLE'S MEDICAL SOCIETY
462 Walnut St.
Allentown, PA 18102
Phone: 215-770-1670

PREVENT BLINDNESS AMERICA
500 E. Remington Rd.
Schaumburg, IL 60173
Phone: 847-843-2020
Toll free: 800-331-2020

SENIORNET
1 Kearney St., 3rd Fl.
San Francisco, CA 94108
Phone: 415-352-1210
Toll free: 800-747-6848 (teaches computer skills to seniors)

SOCIAL SECURITY ADMINISTRATION
Office of Public Inquiries
6401 Security Blvd.
Baltimore, MD 21235
Phone: 410-965-7700
Toll free: 800-772-1213

UNITED PARKINSON FOUNDATION
833 W. Washington Blvd.
Chicago, IL 60607
Phone: 312-664-2344

VISITING NURSE ASSOCIATIONS OF AMERICA
3801 E. Florida, Ste. 900
Denver, CO 80210
Phone: 303-753-0218
Toll free: 800-426-2547

ADDITIONAL TOLL FREE NUMBERS

ELDERCARE LOCATOR
Toll free: 800-677-1116 (makes referrals to local senior resources)

EMERGENCY HUNGER LIFELINE
Toll free: 800-486-4792 (nationwide referrals to the nearest food assistance center)

FUNERAL SERVICE CONSUMER ARBITRATION PROGRAM
Toll free: 800-424-1040

WOMEN'S BUREAU CLEARINGHOUSE
Toll free: 800-827-5335 (information on childcare, eldercare and more)

LEGAL HELP & HOTLINES

You can write to the following organizations for more information on elder law issues or for a referral to an estate planning or elder law attorney in your area:

American College of Trust and Estate Counsel
3415 Sepulveda Blvd., Ste. 460
Los Angeles, CA 90034
Phone: 310-572-7280

HALT, Inc.
1612 K St., NW, Ste. 510
Washington, DC 20006
Phone: 202-887-8255
Toll free: 888-FOR-HALT
URL: http://www.halt.org

National Academy of Elder Law Attorneys
1604 Country Club Rd.
Tucson, AZ 85716
Phone: 520-881-4005

LEGAL HOTLINES

If you are 60 years of age or older you may qualify for free legal assistance over the telephone. A growing number of states now sponsor "legal hotlines" which are designed to expand or improve the delivery of legal assistance to older individuals with social or economic needs. Most are funded through Congressional funds under the Older Americans Act. Some are supported by the Legal Services Corporation, others by state bar funding.

Attorneys staffing the hotlines answer legal questions and give legal advice. They are members of the state bar of the jurisdiction in which the hotline operates. Service is limited to phone advice, but some hotlines will agree to providing additional small services such as reviewing a document or writing a letter, though a fee may be charged for such service. If you need to see an attorney in-person, the hotlines may be able to refer you to lawyers or law firms where appropriate. Ask if there are any fees involved in receiving a referral.

The general requirement for use of the hotlines are you must be 60 years of age or older and live within the state. Most of the services are free and offered through toll free numbers (either 800 or 888). Those that charge, or require qualifications more than being age 60 or over, are noted in their listing below.

CALIFORNIA

Toll free: 800-222-1753 (CA only)
Phone: 916-442-1212
(Sacramento/Out-of-State)

DISTRICT OF COLUMBIA

Phone: 202-434-2170
Note: Service is free to those with a total monthly income under $1,350 (slightly higher for larger households), otherwise, $20 per call.

FLORIDA

Phone: 305-576-5997
Note: Free only to Dade County residents whose income is under $15,000 annually. Otherwise $15.00 per call, plus collect callback.

GEORGIA

Phone: 404-614-3990

HAWAII

Toll free: 888-536-0011
(all islands except Oahu)
Phone: 808-536-0011
(Oahu/Out-of-State)

KANSAS

Toll free: 888-353-5337
Phone: 316-265-9681
(Wichita/Out-of-State)

MAINE

Toll free: 800-750-5353
Phone: 207-623-1797
(Augusta/Out-of-State)

MICHIGAN

Toll free: 800-347-5297
Phone: 517-372-5959
(Lansing/Out-of-State)

MISSISSIPPI

Toll free: 888-660-0008
Phone: 601-374-4160

NEW MEXICO

Toll free: 800-876-6657
Phone: 505-797-6005
(Albuquerque/Out-of-State)

OHIO

Toll free: 800-488-6070
Phone: 513-621-872
(Hamilton County/Out-of-State)

PENNSYLVANIA

Toll free: 800-262-5297
Phone: 412-261-5297
(Allegheny County/Out-of-State)
Notes: $15.00 per call charge if between the ages of 50 and 60 and also to callers whose annual income is over $15,000.

PUERTO RICO

Toll free: 800-981-9160 or 800-981-3432
Phone: 787-728-2323 (Out-of-State)

TEXAS

Toll free: 800-622-2520
Phone: 512-477-3950
(Travis County/Out-of-State)

WASHINGTON

Phone: 206-464-1519

WEST VIRGINIA

Toll free: 800-229-5068
Phone: 304-291-3900
(Morgantown/Out-of-State)

WEB SITES

Alzheimer's Association
URL: http://www.alz.org/
This web site features information on the association, the latest news on Alzheimer's, and a schedule of the association's conferences and events.

American Association of Retired Persons (AARP)
URL: http://www.aarp.org/
AARP site offers consumer health care guides, surveys, schedule of AARP chats on America Online and information on the AARP and membership.

Bet Tzedek
URL: http://comquest1.comquest.com/bet-tzedek/
Bet Tzedek Legal Services is a non-profit public interest law firm which provides free legal services to the elderly and indigent of Los Angeles County. Site has On-Line Guides to Social Security Programs, Medicare and Nursing Home Law (including Medic-aid Eligibility Rules).

California Advocates for Nursing Home Reform (CANHR)
URL: http://www.canhr.org/
Web site features information on CANHR services such as their Legal Information Network and Lawyer Referral Service. Site contains information on the organization and membership, publications and conferences.

Choice in Dying
URL: http://www.choices.org/index.html
The Choice in Dying web site features background information, the latest legal developments and news on the issue of end-of-life care and the right to die. Site also features membership information, publication list and publication order form.

ElderCare
URL: http://www.mindspring.com/~eldrcare/elderweb.htm
This web site is dedicated to helping people navigate the elder care maze. Site features e-mail discussions, caregiver resources, and state-by-state resource directory of elder care service providers.

Eldercare Web
URL: http://www.elderweb.com/
A web site addressing the problems of caring for the elderly. Site contains a collection of articles and links to information related to eldercare, for both providers and consumers of eldercare services.

Funeral and Memorial Societies of America
URL: http://funerals.org/
The only organization monitoring the funeral industry for consumers. Site provides information about the consumer's right to choose a meaningful, dignified and affordable funeral. Links to memorial societies and other death-related web sites.

Insure Market
URL: http://www.insuremarket.com/
Comprehensive information about life, auto, and home insurance and valuable planning strategies to prepare for one's life. Connect with agents, compare quotes and purchase policies from the nation's leading insurance companies.

National Hospice Organization
URL: http://www.nho.org/
Web site offers background and general information on the NHO. Also available on the web site is a listing of NHO conferences and membership information. Member only section features discussion groups, job bank, NHO publications and the most current update on legislative issues affecting hospice-care.

National Institute on Aging
URL: http://www.nih.gov/nia/
NIA web site features the latest news, press releases, announcements, upcoming events and media advisories from NIA-supported research. Site provides information on current NIA research and allows you to order NIA publications on health and aging topics with an online ordering form.

The National Senior Citizens Law Center
URL: http://www.nsclc.org/
The National Senior Citizens Law Center works on areas that affect the security and welfare of older persons of limited income. The NSCLC responds to 4,000 requests for legal assistance annually. NSCLC attorneys are available to serve in a purely supportive or advisory capacity, as active co-council, or as lead counsel in litigation and administrative aging matters.

SeniorLaw
URL: http://www.seniorlaw.com/
Web site where senior citizens, their families, social workers, and financial planners, can access information about Elder Law, Medicare, Medicaid, estate planning, trusts and the rights of the elderly and disabled.

SeniorNet
URL: http://www.seniornet.org/
AOL keyword: SeniorNet
SeniorNet is a national nonprofit organization with the mission of building a community of computer-using seniors. Web and AOL sites have message boards and chat rooms for older adults. SeniorNet has over 100 SeniorNet Learning Centers around the country and publishes computer-related materials for members.

ThirdAge
URL: http://www.thirdage.com/
A Web community of active older adults, 50+ and seniors. Site contains information on health care, computers, retirement, investing, caregiving, travel and much more.

2

HELP FROM
THE GOVERNMENT

If you've ever contacted a government agency—federal, state or local—with a question, you probably already know that getting answers can be easy and tremendously helpful, frustrating and unhelpful, or completely futile.

This chapter tries to clear the way for you. It can't answer your questions, but it can help you find those answers with a little less frustration. It lists the most frequently called federal agencies, and offers you a "Federal Government Hotline" list of toll free numbers for specific programs. It also includes the offices of state attorneys general, governors and secretaries of state, key places you will want to contact for answers to some common problems. The web sites listed at the end of the chapter include the Internet addresses of more than 30 government homepages. If you have access to the Internet, check the appropriate agency's web site for answers to your questions.

No one knows exactly how big the federal government phone world is, but the following statistics give some indication. The Internal Revenue Service alone handled 45 million calls during Fiscal Year 1997. The Immigration and Naturalization Service took about 12 million calls, and the Social Security Administration took 1.5 million calls.

To see what the everyday caller to the government endures, two *Washington Post* reporters recently went "undercover." For two weeks they tried to get answers to 50 tough questions they believed "government agencies should be able to answer."

Their experiences varied. They found some amazing government workers who responded definitively and quickly, but they also found deadbeats "like the self-important General Accounting Office lawyer who, after ignoring voice mail messages for a week, explained blandly that 'if questions are time-sensitive, we rely on callers to call back.'" It's not surprising that more than 30 million callers last year simply gave up. Even so, of the 50 questions asked by the reporters, all but 10 ultimately were answered, the majority in 3 calls or less. So, by all means call and ask your question and remember, if you don't get the answer on the first try, it pays to be persistent.

With government downsizing and wider use of e-mail, voice mail and automated hotlines, some callers feel as though they're caught in an endless and intricate loop that never takes them to a live person or to the answer to their question. To make your visit to federal government agencies more fruitful, here are some helpful hints:

• Identify the correct office to call. If you need help finding out which is the right one for you, start with your local telephone directory. Many have an "Easy Reference List" of topic-specific listings for both state and federal agencies. You can also get referral information and help on the Federal Information Center (FIC) toll free line, **1-800-688-9889**.

• Write down the name and telephone number of everyone you talk with or are referred to. Save the list. Consider it a roadmap to where you have gone in your search for answers; you may need to retrace your steps to take a different route. You're also more likely to get results if the person you're talking with knows you have his or her name.

• When leaving voice mail messages, be sure to include your complete question, name, telephone number(s) and the best times you can be reached. But don't tell your entire problem history: most voice mail systems will end your connection after 30 seconds or a minute, anyway. Besides, brevity will get you a return call a lot more quickly than an overload of details.

• If you keep coming up short, try to win over the next person you speak to by explaining your experience thus far and your desperate need for help.

• If all else fails, ask for the supervisor.

SELECTED FEDERAL AGENCIES

Many federal agencies have enforcement and/or complaint-handling duties for products and services used by the general public. Others act for the benefit of the public, but do not resolve individual consumer problems.

Agencies also have fact sheets, booklets and other information which might be helpful in making purchase decisions and dealing with consumer problems. Numbers for text telephones (TDD/TTY) are included where available. For information about federal agency web sites, see the last section of this chapter.

If you need help in deciding whom to contact with your consumer problem, call the Federal Information Center (FIC) toll free on **1-800-688-9889**.

The list of selected federal agencies is excerpted, in part, from the *1997 Consumer Resource Handbook*, published by the U.S. Office of Consumer Affairs.

COMMISSION ON CIVIL RIGHTS

624 9th St., NW
Washington, DC 20425
Phone: 202-376-8513
(complaint referral in DC)
Toll free: 800-552-6843
(complaint referral outside DC)
TDD nationwide: 202-376-8116
(complaint referral)
Phone: 202-376-8128 (publications)
Phone: 202-376-8312 (public affairs)

COMMODITY FUTURES TRADING COMMISSION

Lafayette Ctr.
1155 21st St., NW
Washington, DC 20581
Phone: 202-418-5506
(complaints)

Phone: 202-418-5080
(information)
TDD: 202-418-5514
(complaints)
TDD: 202-418-5515
(information)

U.S. CONSUMER PRODUCT SAFETY COMMISSION

Washington, DC 20207
Toll free: 800-638-CPSC (2772)
(Product Safety Hotline)
TDD Toll free: 800-638-8270
E-mail: info@cpsc.gov
Fax-on-demand: 301-504-0051

Call the CPSC hotline to report a hazardous product or product-related injury weekdays from 8:30 a.m. to 5 p.m. Recorded messages on safety recommendations and product recalls are available 24 hours a day, 7 days a week.

DEPARTMENT OF COMMERCE

Bureau of the Census
Customer Services
Washington, DC 20233
Phone: 301-457-4100
Fax: 301-457-4714
Fax-on-demand: 900-555-2FAX

Office of Consumer Affairs
Department of Commerce
Rm. 5718
Washington, DC 20230
Phone: 202-482-5001
Fax: 202-482-6007
Fax-on-demand: 202-501-1191
E-mail: CAffairs@doc.gov

National Weather Service
Constituent Affairs
Washington, DC 20230
Phone: 202-482-6090
Fax: 202-482-3154

Patent and Trademark Office
2121 Crystal Dr., Ste. 0100
Arlington, VA 22202
Phone: 703-305-8341
Fax: 703-308-5258

DEPARTMENT OF DEFENSE

Office of National Ombudsman
National Committee for
Employer Support
of the Guard and Reserve
1555 Wilson Blvd., Ste. 200
Arlington, VA 22209-2405
Phone: 703-696-1391
Toll free outside DC:
800-336-4590

Provides assistance with employer/employee problems for members of the Guard and Reserve and their employers.

DEPARTMENT OF EDUCATION

Clearinghouse on Disability
Information
Department of Education
330 C St., SW, Rm. 3132
Washington, DC 20202-2524
Phone/TDD: 202-205-8241

National Clearinghouse on
Bilingual Education Hotline
Department of Education
1118 22nd St., NW
Washington, DC 20037
Phone: 202-467-0867
Toll free outside DC:
800-321-NCBE

Student Financial Aid
Information
Department of Education
P.O. Box 84
Washington, DC 20044
Toll free: 800-4FED-AID (433-3243)
(For general information on student loans, grants and scholarships available from the Department of Education.) For questions on a defaulted account, call the Default Line: Toll free 800-621-3115.

DEPARTMENT OF ENERGY

Department of Energy
P.O. Box 3048
Merrifield, VA 22116
Toll free: 800-363-3732
TDD Toll free: 800-273-2957
BBS: 800-273-2955
E-mail: doe.erec@nciinc.com
For information about conservation and renewable energy or for inquiries about weatherization assistance:

Office of Energy Efficiency and
Renewable Energy
Department of Energy
Washington, DC 20585
Phone: 202-586-4074

**DEPARTMENT OF HEALTH AND
HUMAN SERVICES**

Food and Drug Administration
Dept. of Health and Human Services
5600 Fishers Ln., Rm. 16-75
Rockville, MD 20857
Phone: 301-443-3170 or
Toll free: 800-532-4440

Health Care Financing Administration
Division of Beneficiary Services
Dept. of Health and Human Services
6325 Security Blvd.
Baltimore, MD 21207
Toll free: 800-638-6833
(This is a taped answering service; a
specialist will return your call.)

National Health Information Center
Dept. of Health and Human Services
P.O. Box 1133
Washington, DC 20013-1133
Phone: 301-565-4167 (DC Metro Area)
Toll free: 800-336-4797

Office of Child Support Enforcement
Dept. of Health and Human Services
Washington, DC 20447
Phone: 202-401-9373

Office for Civil Rights
Dept. of Health and Human Services
Washington, DC 20201
Phone: 202-619-0403
Phone: 215-546-1570 (Spanish)
Toll free outside DC: 800-368-1019
TDD Toll free: 800-537-7697

Office of Managed Care
HCFA
Dept. of Health and Human Services
7500 Security Blvd.
Baltimore, MD 21244
Phone: 410-786-4287
Medicare Hotline toll free: 800-638-6833

President's Council on
Physical Fitness and Sports
Dept. of Health and Human Services
701 Pennsylvania Ave., NW, Ste. 250
Washington, DC 20004
Phone: 202-272-3421

DEPARTMENT OF JUSTICE

Antitrust Division
Department of Justice
Washington, DC 20530
Phone: 202-514-2401

Civil Rights Division
Department of Justice
Washington, DC 20530
Phone: 202-514-2151

Federal Bureau of Investigation
Department of Justice
Washington, DC 20535
Phone: 202-324-3000

Immigration and Naturalization Service
Department of Justice
425 I St., NW
Washington, DC 20536
Phone: 202-514-2648
TDD: 202-514-0139

DEPARTMENT OF LABOR

Office of Public Affairs
Department of Labor
Washington, DC 20210
Phone: 202-219-7316 (general inquiries)

Occupational Safety and Health
Administration
Office of Information
& Consumer Affairs
Department of Labor
Washington, DC 20210
Phone: 202-219-8148

Pension and Welfare Benefits
Administration
Office of Program Services
Department of Labor
Washington, DC 20210
Phone: 202-219-8776

DEPARTMENT OF STATE

Bureau of Consular Affairs
Overseas Citizens Services
Department of State
Washington, DC 20520
Phone: 202-647-5225 (emergencies
and non-emergencies, Mon.-Fri., 8:15
a.m.-10 p.m.)

(After hours emergencies, Sundays,
holidays, call 202-647-4000 and ask for
duty officer.)

Passport Services
Washington Passport Agency
1111 19th St., NW
Washington, DC 20524
Phone: 202-647-0518

Visa Services
Department of State
Washington, DC 20520
Phone: 202-663-1225

DEPARTMENT OF TRANSPORTATION

Auto Safety Hotline and
Fax-on-Demand Service
National Highway Traffic Safety
Administration (NHTSA)
Washington, DC 20590
Phone: 202-366-0123
Toll free outside DC: 800-424-9393
TDD: 202-366-7899
TDD toll free outside DC: 800-424-9153

INTERNAL REVENUE SERVICE

Look in your telephone directory under "U.S. Government, Treasury Department, Internal Revenue Service." If it does not appear, call the Federal Information Center toll free on 800-688-9889 or call: Toll free: 800-829-1040 (information and problem resolution).

DEPARTMENT OF VETERANS AFFAIRS

For information about benefits:
Veterans Benefits Administration
Department of Veterans Affairs
810 Vermont Ave., NW
Washington, DC 20420
Toll free: 800-827-1000

For information about medical care:
Veterans Health Administration
810 Vermont Ave., NW
Washington, DC 20420
Phone: 202-273-8952

For information about burials, headstones or markers, and presidential memorial certificates:
National Cemetery System
Department of Veterans Affairs
810 Vermont Ave., NW
Washington, DC 20420
Phone: 202-273-5221

For consumer information or general assistance:
Consumer Affairs Service
Department of Veterans Affairs
810 Vermont Ave., NW
Washington, DC 20420
Phone: 202-273-5760

EQUAL EMPLOYMENT OPPORTUNITY COMMISSION

Office of Communications and
Legislative Affairs
1801 L St., NW
Washington, DC 20507
Phone: 202-663-4900
Toll free outside DC area: 800-669-4000 (file-a-charge information)
Toll free: 800-669-3362 (publications)
TDD Toll free outside DC area: 800-669-6820 (file-a-charge information)
TDD toll free: 800-669-3302 (publications)

FEDERAL COMMUNICATIONS COMMISSION

General information:
Public Services Division
Federal Communications Commission
1919 M St., NW, Rm. 254
Washington, DC 20554
Phone: 202-418-0200
Toll free: 888-322-8255
TTY: 202-418-2555
E-mail: fccinfo@fcc.gov

Complaints about telephone systems:
Common Carrier Bureau
Consumer Protection Division
Federal Communications Commission
2025 M St., NW, Rm. 6202
Washington, DC 20554
Phone: 202-632-7553

Complaints about radio or television:
Mass Media Bureau
Enforcement Division
Federal Communications Commission
2025 M St., NW, Rm. 8210
Washington, DC 20554
Phone: 202-418-1430

Cable service:
Federal Communications Commission
2033 M St., NW
Washington, DC 20036
Phone: 202-418-7096

FEDERAL DEPOSIT INSURANCE CORPORATION

FDIC handles questions about deposit insurance coverage and complaints about FDIC- insured state banks which are not members of the Federal Reserve System. For assistance, look in your telephone directory under "U.S. Government, Federal Deposit Insurance Corporation." If it does not appear, call the Federal Information Center toll free on 800-688-9889 or contact:

Division of Compliance and Consumer Affairs Federal Deposit Insurance Corporation
550 17th St., NW
Washington, DC 20429-9990
Phone: 202-942-3100
Toll free: 800-934-3342

FEDERAL TRADE COMMISSION

Correspondence Branch
Federal Trade Commission
Washington, DC 20580
(written complaints only)

Public Reference Section
Federal Trade Commission
6th & Pennsylvania Ave., NW, Rm. 130
Washington, DC 20580
Phone: 202-326-2222 (publications)

GOVERNMENT PRINTING OFFICE

Government Printing Office
P.O. Box 371954
Pittsburgh, PA 15250-7954
Phone: 202-512-1800

PENSION BENEFIT GUARANTY CORPORATION

Customer Service Center
1200 K St., NW
Washington, DC 20005
Phone: 202-326-4000
TDD: 202-326-4179

POSTAL RATE COMMISSION

1333 H St., NW, Ste. 300
Washington, DC 20268
Phone: 202-789-6830

POSTAL SERVICE

If you experience difficulty when ordering merchandise or conducting business transactions through the mail, or suspect that you have been the victim of a mail fraud or misrepresentation scheme, contact your postmaster or local Postal Inspector. Look in your telephone directory under "U.S. Government, Postal Service U.S." for these local listings. If they do not appear, contact:

Chief Postal Inspector
U.S. Postal Service
Washington, DC 20260-2100
Phone: 202-268-2284

For consumer convenience, all post offices and letter carriers have postage-free Consumer Service Cards available for reporting mail problems and submitting comments and suggestions.

If the problem cannot be resolved using the Consumer Service Card or through direct contact with the local post office, write or call:

Consumer Advocate
United States Postal Service
Washington, DC 20260-2200
Phone: 202-268-2284
TDD: 202-268-2310

RAILROAD RETIREMENT BOARD

844 N. Rush St.
Chicago, IL 60611-2092
Phone: 312-751-4500

SECURITIES AND EXCHANGE COMMISSION

450 5th St., NW
Mail Stop 11-2
Washington, DC 20549
Phone: 202-942-7040
Fax: 202-942-9634
E-mail: help@sec.gov
For information and to order publications: Toll free: 800-SEC-0330

SMALL BUSINESS ADMINISTRATION

Consumer Affairs
409 3rd St., SW
Washington, DC 20416
Toll free: 800-U-ASK-SBA (information)

SOCIAL SECURITY ADMINISTRATION

Office of Public Inquiries
6401 Security Blvd.
Baltimore, MD 21235
Toll free: 800-772-1213

ATTORNEYS GENERAL

If you have a problem with a state government agency, or want to report an illegal activity by an agency, employee or official of the state, call the office of your state's attorney general. The attorney general is the state's chief lawyer and law officer. That means it's his or her job to represent your state in court in all matters in which the state has an interest or is named as a party.

In most states, the attorney general is responsible for the state's consumer protection programs (Chapter 3). The office is also responsible for criminal investigations not handled by the state's attorney.

ALABAMA

Hon. Bill Pryor
Attorney General of Alabama
Office of the Attorney General
State House, 11 S. Union St.
Montgomery, AL 36130
Phone: 334-242-7300

ALASKA

Hon. Bruce M. Botelho
Attorney General of Alaska
Office of the Attorney General
P.O. Box 110300
Diamond Courthouse
Juneau, AK 99811-0300
Phone: 907-465-3600

ARIZONA

Hon. Grant Woods
Attorney General of Arizona
Office of the Attorney General
1275 W. Washington St.
Phoenix, AZ 85007
Phone: 602-542-4266

ARKANSAS

Hon. Winston Bryant
Attorney General of Arkansas
Office of the Attorney General
200 Tower Bldg., 323 Ctr. St.
Little Rock, AR 72201-2610
Phone: 501-682-2007

CALIFORNIA

Hon. Daniel Lungren
Attorney General of California
Office of the Attorney General
1300 I St., Ste. 1740
Sacramento, CA 95814
Phone: 916-324-5437

COLORADO

Hon. Gale Norton
Attorney General of Colorado
Office of the Attorney General
Department of Law
1525 Sherman St.
Denver, CO 80203
Phone: 303-866-3052

CONNECTICUT

Hon. Richard Blumenthal
Attorney General of Connecticut
Office of the Attorney General
55 Elm St.
Hartford, CT 06141-0120
Phone: 860-566-2026

DELAWARE

Hon. M. Jane Brady
Attorney General of Delaware
Office of the Attorney General
Carvel State Office Bldg.
820 N. French St.
Wilmington, DE 19801
Phone: 302-577-3838

DISTRICT OF COLUMBIA

Hon. Jo Anne Robinson
Acting Director
Office of the Corporation Counsel
441 4th St., NW
Washington, DC 20001
Phone: 202-727-6248

FLORIDA

Hon. Robert Butterworth
Attorney General of Florida
Office of the Attorney General
The Capitol, PL 01
Tallahassee, FL 32399-1050
Phone: 904-487-1963

GEORGIA

Hon. Thurbert E. Baker
Attorney General of Georgia
Office of the Attorney General
40 Capitol Sq., SW
Atlanta, GA 30334-1300
Phone: 404-656-4585

HAWAII

Hon. Margery Bronster
Attorney General of Hawaii
Office of the Attorney General
425 Queen St.
Honolulu, HI 96813
Phone: 808-586-1282

IDAHO

Hon. Alan G. Lance
Attorney General of Idaho
Office of the Attorney General
Statehouse
Boise, ID 83720-1000
Phone: 208-334-2400

ILLINOIS

Hon. Jim Ryan
Attorney General of Illinois
Office of the Attorney General
James R. Thompson Ctr.
100 W. Randolph St.
Chicago, IL 60601
Phone: 312-814-2503

INDIANA

Hon. Jeffrey Modisett
Attorney General of Indiana
Office of the Attorney General
Indiana Government Ctr. South
402 W. Washington St., 5th Fl.
Indianapolis, IN 46204
Phone: 317-233-4386

IOWA

Hon. Tom Miller
Attorney General of Iowa
Office of the Attorney General
Hoover State Office Bldg.
Des Moines, IA 50319
Phone: 515-281-3053

KANSAS

Hon. Carla Stovall
Attorney General of Kansas
Office of the Attorney General
Judicial Bldg.
301 W. Tenth St.
Topeka, KS 66612-1597
Phone: 913-296-2215

KENTUCKY

Hon. Albert Benjamin Chandler III
Attorney General of Kentucky
Office of the Attorney General
State Capitol, Rm. 116
Frankfort, KY 40601
Phone: 502-564-7600

LOUISIANA

Hon. Richard Ieyoub
Attorney General of Louisiana
Office of the Attorney General
Department of Justice
P.O. Box 94095
Baton Rouge, LA 70804-4095
Phone: 504-342-7013

MAINE

Hon. Andrew Ketterer
Attorney General of Maine
Office of the Attorney General
State House Station Six
Augusta, ME 04333
Phone: 207-626-8800

MARYLAND

Hon. J. Joseph Curran Jr.
Attorney General of Maryland
Office of the Attorney General
200 St. Paul Pl.
Baltimore, MD 21202-2202
Phone: 410-576-6300

MASSACHUSETTS

Hon. Scott Harshbarger
Attorney General of Massachusetts
Office of the Attorney General
One Ashburton Pl.
Boston, MA 02108-1698
Phone: 617-727-2200

MICHIGAN

Hon. Frank J. Kelley
Attorney General of Michigan
Office of the Attorney General
P.O. Box 30212
525 W. Ottawa St.
Lansing, MI 48909-0212
Phone: 517-373-1110

MINNESOTA

Hon. Hubert Humphrey III
Attorney General of Minnesota
Office of the Attorney General
State Capitol, Ste. 102
St. Paul, MN 55155
Phone: 612-296-6196

MISSISSIPPI

Hon. Mike Moore
Attorney General of Mississippi
Office of the Attorney General
P.O. Box 220
Jackson, MS 39205-0220
Phone: 601-359-3692

MISSOURI

Hon. Jeremiah W. Nixoino
Attorney General of Missouri
Office of the Attorney General
Supreme Court Bldg.
207 W. High St.
Jefferson City, MO 65101
Phone: 573-751-3321

MONTANA

Hon. Joseph Mazurek
Attorney General of Montana
Office of the Attorney General
Justice Bldg.
215 N. Sanders
Helena, MT 59620-1401
Phone: 406-444-2026

NEBRASKA

Hon. Don Stenberg
Attorney General of Nebraska
Office of the Attorney General
State Capitol
P.O. Box 98920
Lincoln, NE 68509-8920
Phone: 402-471-2682

NEVADA

Hon. Frankie Sue Del Papa
Attorney General of Nevada
Office of the Attorney General
Old Supreme Court Bldg.
198 S. Carson
Carson City, NV 89710
Phone: 702-687-4170

NEW HAMPSHIRE

Hon. Philip McLaughlin
Attorney General of New Hampshire
Office of the Attorney General
State House Annex
25 Capitol St.
Concord, NH 03301-6397
Phone: 609-292-4925

NEW JERSEY

Hon. Peter Verniero
Attorney General of New Jersey
Office of the Attorney General
25 Market St., CN 080
Trenton, NJ 08625
Phone: 609-292-4925

NEW MEXICO

Hon. Tom Udall
Attorney General of New Mexico
Office of the Attorney General
P.O. Drawer 1508
Santa Fe, NM 87504-1508
Phone: 505-827-6000

NEW YORK

Hon. Dennis Vacco
Attorney General of New York
Office of the Attorney General
Department of Law
The Capitol, 2nd Fl.
Albany, NY 12224
Phone: 518-474-7330

NORTH CAROLINA

Hon. Michael Easley
Attorney General of North Carolina
Office of the Attorney General
Department of Justice
P.O. Box 629
Raleigh, NC 27602-0629
Phone: 919-733-3377

NORTH DAKOTA

Hon. Heidi Heitkamp
Attorney General of North Dakota
Office of the Attorney General
State Capitol
600 E. Boulevard Ave.
Bismark, ND 58505-0040
Phone: 701-328-2210

OHIO

Hon. Betty Montgomery
Attorney General of Ohio
Office of the Attorney General
State Office Tower
30 E. Broad St.
Columbus, OH 43266-0410
Phone: 614-466-3376

OKLAHOMA

Hon. Drew Edmondson
Attorney General of Oklahoma
Office of the Attorney General
State Capitol, Rm. 112
2300 N. Lincoln Blvd.
Oklahoma City, OK 73105
Phone: 405-521-3921

OREGON

Hon. Hardy Myers
Attorney General of Oregon
Office of the Attorney General
Justice Bldg., 1162 Court St., NE
Salem, OR 97310
Phone: 503-378-6002

PENNSYLVANIA

Hon. Mike Fisher
Attorney General of Pennsylvania
Office of the Attorney General
Strawberry Sq.
Harrisburg, PA 17120
Phone: 717-787-3391

PUERTO RICO

Hon. Jose Fuentes-Agostini
Attorney General of Puerto Rico
Office of the Attorney General
P.O. Box 192
San Juan, PR 00902-0192
Phone: 787-721-7700

RHODE ISLAND

Hon. Jeffrey Pine
Attorney General of Rhode Island
Office of the Attorney General
150 S. Main St.
Providence, RI 02903
Phone: 401-274-4400

SOUTH CAROLINA

Hon. Charlie Condon
Attorney General of South Carolina
Office of the Attorney General
Rembert Dennis Office Bldg.
P.O. Box 11549
Columbia, SC 29211-1549
Phone: 803-734-3970

SOUTH DAKOTA

Hon. Mark Barnett
Attorney General of South Dakota
Office of the Attorney General
500 E. Capitol
Pierre, SD 57501-5070
Phone: 605-773-3215

TENNESSEE

Hon. John Knox Walkup
Attorney General of Tennessee
Office of the Attorney General
500 Charlotte Ave.
Nashville, TN 37243
Phone: 615-741-6474

TEXAS

Hon. Dan Morales
Attorney General of Texas
Office of the Attorney General
Capitol Station
P.O. Box 12548
Austin, TX 78711-2548
Phone: 512-463-2191

UTAH

Hon. Jan Graham
Attorney General of Utah
Office of the Attorney General
State Capitol, Rm. 236
Salt Lake City, UT 84114-0810
Phone: 801-538-1326

VERMONT

Hon. William Sorrell
Attorney General of Vermont
Office of the Attorney General
109 State St.
Montpelier, VT 05609-1001
Phone: 802-828-3171

VIRGINIA

Hon. Richard Cullen
Attorney General of Virginia
Office of the Attorney General
900 E. Main St.
Richmond, VA 23219
Phone: 804-786-2071

VIRGIN ISLANDS

Hon. Julio Brady
Attorney General of Virgin Islands
Office of the Attorney General
Department of Justice
G.E.R.S. Complex
48B-50C Kronprinsdens Gade
St. Thomas, VI 00802
Phone: 809-774-5666

WASHINGTON

Hon. Christine Gregoire
Attorney General of Washington
Office of the Attorney General
P.O. Box 40100
1125 Washington St., SE
Olympia, WA 98504-0100
Phone: 360-753-6200

WEST VIRGINIA

Hon. Darrell McGraw, Jr.
Attorney General of West Virginia
Office of the Attorney General
State Capitol
Charleston, WV 25305
Phone: 304-558-2021

WISCONSIN

Hon. James Doyle
Attorney General of Wisconsin
Office of the Attorney General
P.O. Box 7857
Madison, WI 53707-7857
Phone: 608-266-1221

WYOMING

Hon. William Hill
Attorney General of Wyoming
Office of the Attorney General
State Capitol Bldg.
Cheyenne, WY 82002
Phone: 307-777-7841

GOVERNORS

As the highest elected official in your state, the governor has the responsibility of running the state. You may not have reason to speak directly to the governor, but at times you may want to make your voice heard outside the voting booth on issues that are important to you as a parent, neighbor, consumer, taxpayer or citizen. For example, you may want to call the governor's office to voice support or opposition to legislation waiting for his or her signature.

The governor's office may be able to help you communicate with state agencies that you're having difficulty getting through to. The governor's office is also an excellent place to call if you don't know which state agency to call about your specific problem. It is almost always the case that someone on the governor's staff will be able to direct you to the appropriate office.

ALABAMA

Gov. Fob James Jr.
State Capitol, 600 Dexter Ave.
Montgomery, AL 36130
Phone: 334-242-7100

ALASKA

Gov. Tony Knowles
P.O. Box 110001
Juneau, AK 99811-0001
Phone: 907-465-3500

ARIZONA

Gov. Jane Hull
State Capitol
1700 W. Washington
Phoenix, AZ 85007
Phone: 602-542-4331

ARKANSAS

Gov. Mike Huckabee
250 State Capitol
Little Rock, AR 72201
Phone: 501-682-2345

CALIFORNIA

Gov. Pete Wilson
State Capitol
Sacramento, CA 95814
Phone: 916-445-2864

COLORADO

Gov. Roy Romer
136 State Capitol
Denver, CO 80203-1792
Phone: 303-866-2471

CONNECTICUT

Gov. John Rowland
210 Capitol Ave.
Hartford, CT 06106
Phone: 203-566-4840

DELAWARE

Gov. Toni Carper
Tatnall Bldg.
William Penn St.
Dover, DE 19901
Phone: 302-739-4101

FLORIDA

Gov. Lawton Chiles
The Capitol
Tallahassee, FL 32399-0001
Phone: 904-488-2272

GEORGIA

Gov. Zell Miller
203 State Capitol
Atlanta, GA 30334
Phone: 404-656-1776

HAWAII

Gov. Benjamin Cayetano
State Capitol
Honolulu, HI 96813
Phone: 808-586-0034

IDAHO

Gov. Philip Batt
State Capitol
Boise, ID 83720-0034
Phone: 208-334-2100

ILLINOIS

Gov. Jim Edgar
State Capitol
Springfield, IL 62706
Phone: 217-782-6830

INDIANA

Gov. Frank O'Bannon
206 State House
Indianapolis, IN 46206
Phone: 317-232-4567

IOWA

Gov. Terry Branstad
State Capitol
Des Moines, IA 50319-0001
Phone: 515-281-5211

KANSAS

Gov. Bill Graves
Capitol Bldg., 2nd Fl.
Topeka, KS 66612-1590
Phone: 913-296-3232

KENTUCKY

Gov. Paul Patton
State Capitol
700 Capitol Ave.
Frankfort, KY 40601
Phone: 502-564-2611

LOUISIANA

Gov. Mike Foster
P.O. Box 94004
Baton Rouge, LA 70804-9004
Phone: 504-342-7015

MAINE

Gov. Angus King Jr.
State House, Station 1
Augusta, ME 04333
Phone: 207-287-3531

MARYLAND

Gov. Parris Glendening
State House
100 State Cir.
Annapolis, MD 21404
Phone: 410-974-3901

MASSACHUSETTS

Gov. Paul Cellucci
State House, Rm. 360
Boston, MA 02133
Phone: 617-727-9173

MICHIGAN

Gov. John Engler
P.O. Box 30013
Lansing, MI 48909
Phone: 517-373-3400

MINNESOTA

Gov. Arne Carlson
130 State Capitol
75 Constitution Ave.
St. Paul, MN 55155
Phone: 612-296-3391

MISSISSIPPI

Gov. Kirk Fordice
P.O. Box 139
Jackson, MS 39205
Phone: 601-359-3150

MISSOURI

Gov. Mel Carnahan
State Capitol, Rm. 216
Jefferson City, MO 65101
Phone: 573-751-3222

MONTANA

Gov. Marc Racicot
State Capitol
Helena, MT 59620-0801
Phone: 406-444-3111

NEBRASKA

Gov. E. Banjamin Nelson
P.O. Box 94848
Lincoln, NE 68509-4848
Phone: 402-471-2244

NEVADA

Gov. Bob Miller
State Capitol
Carson City, NV 89710
Phone: 702-687-5670

NEW HAMPSHIRE

Gov. Jeanne Shaheen
State House, Rm. 208
Concord, NH 03301
Phone: 603-271-2121

NEW JERSEY

Gov. Christine Whitman
125 W. State St.
CN-001
Trenton, NJ 08625
Phone: 609-292-6000

NEW MEXICO

Gov. Gary Johnson
State Capitol, 4th Fl.
Santa Fe, NM 87503
Phone: 505-827-3000

NEW YORK

Gov. Georege Pataki
State Capitol
Albany, NY 12224
Phone: 518-474-7516

NORTH CAROLINA

Gov. James Hunt Jr.
State Capitol
Capitol Square
Raleigh, NC 27603-8001
Phone: 919-733-4240

NORTH DAKOTA

Gov. Edward Schafer
600 E. Boulevard Ave.
Bismarck, ND 58505-0001
Phone: 701-328-2200

OHIO

Gov. George Voinovich
77 S. High St., 30th Fl.
Columbus, OH 43266-0601
Phone: 614-466-3555

OKLAHOMA

Gov. Frank Keating
State Capitol Bldg., Ste. 212
Oklahoma City, OK 73105
Phone: 614-521-2342

OREGON

Gov. John Kitzhaber
254 State Capitol
Salem, OR 97310
Phone: 503-378-3111

PENNSYLVANIA

Gov. Tom Ridge
225 Main Capitol Bldg.
Harrisburg, PA 17120
Phone: 717-787-2500

RHODE ISLAND

Gov. Lincoln Almond
State House
Providence, RI 02903
Phone: 401-277-2080

SOUTH CAROLINA

Gov. David Beasley
P.O. Box 11369
Columbia, SC 29211
Phone: 803-734-9818

SOUTH DAKOTA

Gov. William Janklow
500 E. Capitol
Pierre, SD 57501
Phone: 605-773-3212

TENNESSEE

Gov. Don Sundquist
State Capitol
Nashville, TN 37243-0001
Phone: 615-741-2001

TEXAS

Gov. George Bush
P.O. Box 12428
Austin, TX 78711
Phone: 512-463-2000

UTAH

Gov. Michael Leavitt
State Capitol, Ste. 2100
Salt Lake City, UT 84118
Phone: 801-538-1500

VERMONT

Gov. Howard Dean
Pavilion Office Bldg.
109 State St.
Montpelier, VT 05609
Phone: 802-828-3333

VIRGINIA

Gov. Jim Gilmore
State Capitol
Richmond, VA 23219
Phone: 804-786-2211

WASHINGTON

Gov. Gary Locke
P.O. Box 40002
Legislative Bldg.
Olympia, WA 98504-0002
Phone: 360-753-6780

WEST VIRGINIA

Gov. Cecil Underwood
State Capitol Complex
Charleston, WV 25305-0370
Phone: 304-558-2000

WISCONSIN

Gov. Tommy Thompson
State Capitol
P.O. Box 7863
Madison, WI 53707
Phone: 608-266-1212

WYOMING

Gov. Jim Geringer
State Capitol Bldg., Rm. 124
Cheyenne, WY 82002
Phone: 307-777-7434

SECRETARIES OF STATE

The responsibilities of the secretary of state vary from state to state, but in general this is the office that maintains the state's official records, probably including vehicle titles, drivers' licenses, mandatory vehicle insurance records, voter registrations and state-registered trademarks. The office also is typically responsible for certifying and registering notaries in the state and maintaining records on corporations doing business in the state. Finally, it is charged with assuring proper use and display of the state flag, official seal and other official documents.

Many secretaries of state have expanded roles, including overseeing such educational programs as those about drunk driving, traffic safety, literacy and organ donation. Call your secretary of state's office to learn what it offers.

ALABAMA

Hon. Jim Bennett
State House
600 Dexter Ave.
Montgomery, AL 36130
Phone: 334-242-7205
Fax: 334-242-4993

ALASKA

Hon. Fran Ulmer
P.O. Box 110015
Juneau, AK 99811-0015
Phone: 907-465-3520
Fax: 907-465-5400

ARIZONA

Hon. Jane Dee Hull
State Capitol
1700 W. Washington, 7th Fl.
Phoenix, AZ 85007-2808
Phone: 602-542-3012
Fax: 602-542-1575

ARKANSAS

Hon. Sharon Priest
256 State Capitol Bldg.
Little Rock, AR 72201
Phone: 501-682-1010
Fax: 601-682-3510

CALIFORNIA

Hon. Bill Jones
1500 11th St.
Sacramento, CA 95814
Phone: 916-653-7244
Fax: 916-653-4620

COLORADO

Hon. Vikki Buckley
1560 Broadway, Ste. 200
Denver, CO 80202
Phone: 303-894-2200
Fax: 303-894-7732

CONNECTICUT

Hon. Miles Rapoport
State Capitol, Rm. 104
Hartford, CT 06106
Phone: 860-566-2739
Fax: 860-566-6318

DISTRICT OF COLUMBIA

Hon. Kathleen Arnold
441 4th St., NW, Ste. 1130
Washington, DC 20004
Phone: 202-727-6306
Fax: 202-727-3582

DELAWARE

Hon. Edward Freel
Townsend Bldg.
P.O. Box 898
Dover, DE 19903
Phone: 302-739-4111
Fax: 302-739-3811

FLORIDA

Hon. Sandy Mortham
Capitol Plaza Level, Rm. 2
Tallahassee, FL 32399
Phone: 904-922-0234
Fax: 904-487-2214

GEORGIA

Hon. Lewis Massey
State Capitol, Rm. 214
Atlanta, GA 30334
Phone: 404-656-2881
Fax: 404-657-5804

HAWAII

Hon. Mazie Hirono
State Capitol, 5th Fl.
Honolulu, HI 96813
Phone: 808-586-0255
Fax: 808-586-0231

IDAHO

Hon. Pete Cenarrusa
State Capitol, Rm. 203
Boise, ID 83720
Phone: 208-334-2300
Fax: 208-334-2282

ILLINOIS

Hon. George Ryan, Sr.
213 State Capitol
Springfield, IL 62756
Phone: 217-782-2201
Fax: 217-785-0358

INDIANA

Hon. Sue Ann Gilroy
201 State House
Indianapolis, IN 46204
Phone: 317-232-6531
Fax: 317-233-3283

IOWA

Hon. Paul Pate
State House
Des Moines, IA 50319
Phone: 515-281-5204
Fax: 515-242-5952/5953

KANSAS

Hon. Ron Thornburgh
Capitol, 2nd Fl.
Topeka, KS 66612
Phone: 913-296-4575
Fax: 913-296-4570

KENTUCKY

Hon. John Brown, III
State Capitol, Rm. 150
Frankfort, KY 40601-3493
Phone: 502-564-3490
Fax: 502-564-5687

LOUISIANA

Hon. W. Fox McKeithen
P.O. Box 94125
Baton Rouge, LA 70804
Phone: 504-342-4479
Fax: 504-342-5577

MAINE

Hon. Dan Gwadosky
Nash Bldg., Station #148
Augusta, ME 04333-0148
Phone: 207-626-8400
Fax: 207-287-8598

MARYLAND

Hon. John Willis
State House
Annapolis, MD 21401
Phone: 401-974-5521
Fax: 401-974-5190

MASSACHUSETTS

Hon. William Galvin
State House, Rm. 337
Boston, MA 02133
Phone: 617-727-9180
Fax: 617-742-4722

MICHIGAN

Hon. Candice Miller
Treasury Bldg., 1st Fl.
430 W. Allegan St.
Lansing, MI 48918
Phone: 517-373-2510
Fax: 517-373-0727

MINNESOTA

Hon. Joan Growe
180 State Office Bldg.
100 Constitution Ave.
St. Paul, MN 55155-1299
Phone: 612-296-2079
Fax: 612-297-5844

MISSISSIPPI

Hon. Eric Clark
P.O. Box 136
401 Mississippi St.
Jackson, MS 29205-0136
Phone: 601-359-1350
Fax: 601-354-6243

MISSOURI

Hon. Rebecca Cook
208 State Capitol
P.O. Box 778
Jefferson City, MO 65102
Phone: 573-751-3318
Fax: 573-526-4903

MONTANA

Hon. Mike Cooney
State Capitol, Rm. 225
Helena, MT 59620
Phone: 406-444-2034
Fax: 404-444-3976

NEBRASKA

Hon. Scott Moore
State Capitol, Ste. 2300
P.O. Box 94608
Lincoln, NE 68509-4608
Phone: 402-471-2554
Fax: 402-471-3237

NEVADA

Hon. Dean Heller
Capitol Complex
Carson City, NV 89710
Phone: 702-687-5203
Fax: 702-687-3471

NEW HAMPSHIRE

Hon. William Gardner
State House, Rm. 204
Concord, NH 03301
Phone: 603-271-3242
Fax: 603-271-6316

NEW JERSEY

Hon. Lonna Hooks
CN-300
Trenton, NJ 08625
Phone: 609-984-1900
Fax: 609-292-9897

NEW MEXICO

Hon. Stephanie González
State Capitol, Rm. 420
Santa Fe, NM 87503
Phone: 505-827-3600
Fax: 505-827-3634

NEW YORK

Hon. Alexander Treadwell
162 Washington Ave.
Albany, NY 12231
Phone: 518-474-0050
Fax: 518-474-4765

NORTH CAROLINA

Hon. Elaine Marshall
300 N. Salisbury St.
Raleigh, NC 27603-5909
Phone: 919-733-5140
Fax: 919-733-4092

NORTH DAKOTA

Hon. Alvin Jaeger
State Capitol
600 E. Boulevard, 1st Fl.
Bismarck, ND 58505-0500
Phone: 701-328-2900
Fax: 701-328-2992

OHIO

Hon. Bob Taft
30 E. Broad St., 14th Fl.
Columbus, OH 43299-0418
Phone: 614-466-2655
Fax: 614-644-0649

OKLAHOMA

Hon. Tom Cole
State Capitol, Rm. 101
Oklahoma City, OK 73105
Phone: 405-521-3911
Fax: 405-521-3771

OREGON

Hon. Phil Keisling
136 State Capitol
Salem, OR 97310
Phone: 503-986-1523
Fax: 503-986-1616

PENNSYLVANIA

Hon. Yvette Kane
302 N. Capitol Bldg.
Harrisburg, PA 17120
Phone: 717-787-7630
Fax: 717-787-1734

RHODE ISLAND

Hon. James Langevin
218 State House
Providence, RI 02903
Phone: 401-277-2357
Fax: 401-277-1356

SOUTH CAROLINA

Hon. Jim Miles
Wade Hampton Bldg.
P.O. Box 11350
Columbia, SC 29211
Phone: 803-734-2170
Fax: 803-734-2164

SOUTH DAKOTA

Hon. Joyce Hazeltine
500 E. Capitol Bldg., Ste. 204
Pierre, SD 57501
Phone: 605-773-3537
Fax: 605-773-6580

TENNESSEE

Hon. Riley Darnell
State Capitol, 1st Fl.
Nashville, TN 37243-0350
Phone: 615-741-2819
Fax: 615-741-5962

TEXAS

Hon. Tony Garza
State Capitol, 1E.8
1200 Congress Ave.
P.O. Box 12697
Austin, TX 78711
Phone: 512-463-5701
Fax: 512-475-2761

UTAH

Hon. Olene Walker
203 State Capitol Bldg.
Salt Lake City, UT 84114
Phone: 801-538-1520
Fax: 801-538-1557

VERMONT

Hon. James Milne
109 State St.
Montpelier, VT 05609-1101
Phone: 802-828-2148
Fax: 802-828-2496

VIRGINIA

Hon. Betsy Davis Beamer
P.O. Box 2454
Capitol Sq.
Richmond, VA 23201
Phone: 804-786-2441
Fax: 804-371-0017

WASHINGTON

Hon. Ralph Munro
Legislative Bldg., 2nd Fl.
P.O. Box 40220
Olympia, WA 98504-0220
Phone: 360-753-7121
Fax: 360-586-5629

WEST VIRGINIA

Hon. Ken Hechler
Bldg. 1
1900 Kanawha Blvd., East, Ste. 157K
Charleston, WV 25305
Phone: 304-558-6000
Fax: 304-558-0900

WISCONSIN

Hon. Douglas La Follette
30 W. Mifflin St.,
9th and 10th Fl.
Madison, WI 53703
Phone: 608-266-8888
Fax: 608-266-3159

WYOMING

Hon. Diana Ohman
State Capitol Bldg.
Cheyenne, WY 82002
Phone: 307-777-5333
Fax: 307-777-6217

FEDERAL TOLL FREE NUMBERS

If you need help in deciding whom to contact with your consumer problem, call the Federal Information Center (FIC) toll free at **1-800-688-9889**.

AIDS HOTLINE
Toll free: 800-342-AIDS (24 hrs.)
Toll free: 800-344-SIDA

AIR SAFETY
Toll free: 800-255-1111 (safety hotline)

AUTO SAFETY HOTLINE
Toll free: 800-424-9393

BLIND & PHYSICALLY HANDICAPPED
Toll free: 800-424-9100

BOATING SAFETY HOTLINE
Toll free: 800-368-5647

CANCER HOTLINE
Toll free: 800-4-CANCER

CHILD ABUSE HOTLINE
Toll free: 800-394-3366

CONSUMER PRODUCT SAFETY COMMISSION
Toll free: 800-638-CPSC

FAIR HOUSING & EQUAL OPPORTUNITY
Toll free: 800 669-9777

FEDERAL AVIATION ADMINISTRATION
Toll free: 800-FAA-SURE

FEDERAL COMMUNICATIONS COMMISSION
Toll free: 888-322-8255

FREE HOSPITAL CARE HOTLINE
Toll free: 800-492-0359 (in MD)
Toll free: 800-638-0742 (outside MD)

INTERNAL REVENUE SERVICE
Toll free: 800-829-1040

MEAT & POULTRY HOTLINE FOOD SAFETY & INSPECTION SERVICE
Toll free: 800-535-4555

MEDICARE HOTLINE
Toll free: 800-638-6833

NATIONAL RUNAWAY SWITCHBOARD
Toll free: 800-621-4000

OIL AND CHEMICAL SPILLS
Toll free: 800-424-8802

SAFE DRINKING WATER HOTLINE
Toll free: 800-426-4791

SMALL BUSINESS ADMINISTRATION
Toll free: 800-U-ASK-SBA

SOCIAL SECURITY ADMINISTRATION
Toll free: 800-772-1213

STUDENT FINANCIAL AID INFORMATION
Toll free: 800-4FED-A
Defaulted account, call: 800-621-3115

U.S. SAVINGS BONDS
Toll free: 800-4US-BOND

VETERANS BENEFITS ADMINISTRATION
Toll free: 800-827-1000

WOMEN'S BUREAU INFORMATION
Toll free: 800-827-5335

WEB SITES

Bureau of Alcohol, Tobacco and Firearms
URL: http://www.atf.treas.gov/
BATF's site offers information on the Bureau, the BATF's most wanted, forms, publications and other BATF news.

Central Intelligence Agency
URL: http://www.odci.gov/cia/index.html
CIA's site presents all you ever wanted to know about the CIA, CIA publications, press releases, statements, speeches and testimony.

Consumer Information Center
URL: http://www.pueblo.gsa.gov/
At this site you can view the complete text editions of 200 of the best publications from the Federal government. You can also browse the Consumer Information Catalog, read consumer news, see special publications of consumer interest, and either order a printed copy of the Consumer Information Catalog or download it.

Consumer Product Safety Commission
URL: http://www.cpsc.gov/
The web site to visit for information that keeps American families safe by reducing the risk of injury or death from consumer products. Visit the CPSC site to report unsafe products and find out about the latest product recalls.

Department of Agriculture
URL: http://www.usda.gov/
Web site features the latest USDA news and information and links to the agencies under the USDA such as the Farm Service Agency, the Animal and Plant Health Inspection Service, Forest Service, and the Rural Utilities Services.

Department of Health and Human Services
URL: http://www.os.dhhs.gov/
HHS web site features electronic public service announcements, HHS news and public affairs, and the healthfinder™ gateway which provides links to sites that offer health-related information that can help you make better choices for you and your family's health and human services needs.

Department of Justice
URL: http://www.usdoj.gov/
Information on the largest law firm in the nation. Site offers Justice Department news, issues, topics of interest and links to Justice Department organizations.

Department of State
URL: http://www.state.gov/
State Department's web site offers information on travel, travel warnings, foreign offices, living overseas as well as department policy, news and activities. Also available on site are downloadable passport applications and other information on passport services.

Department of Transportation
URL: http://www.dot.gov/
The DOT web site provides access to the National Transportation Library as well as transportation news, statistics, legislation and regulation, and safety issues.

Department of the Treasury
URL: http://www.ustreas.gov/
The Treasury web site offers information on the Treasury Department, including tour information.

Department of Veterans Affairs
URL: http://www.va.gov/
The VA web site features press releases, benefits information, facilities, special programs and much more.

Environmental Protection Agency
URL: http://www.epa.gov/
The EPA web site features information on the agency, EPA news and events, environmental laws and regulations, and tips for environmentally-conscious consumers.

Equal Employment Opportunity Commission
URL: http://www.eeoc.gov/
The EEOC web site includes information about the Commission, facts about employment discrimination, filing a charge, enforcement and litigation.

Federal Bureau of Investigation
URL: http://www.fbi.gov/
The FBI web site features information on the FBI and its history, the FBI's most wanted, major investigations, crime alert, programs, publications, tours and much more.

Federal Communications Commission
URL: http://www.fcc.gov/
FCC web site features FCC Daily Digest, auctions, consumer information, forms, fees, information on acts and rulemakings.

Federal Trade Commission
URL: http://www.ftc.gov/
FTC web site offers information on the FTC, facts for consumers and businesses, consumer protection rules and guidelines, commission action reports, news releases and information on how to report fraud.

Food and Drug Administration
URL: http://www.fda.gov/
FDA site offers news and information on a wide variety of topics related to the FDA's work such as drugs, biologics, medical devices and toxicology. Site also features information on MedWatch, the FDA Medical Products Reporting Program and offers instructions on how to report adverse drug reactions and medical product problems to the FDA.

Immigration and Naturalization Service
URL: http://www.ins.usdoj.gov/
INS web site offers information on the agency, immigration law and regulations, downloadable forms, employer information, media releases, statistics and more.

Internal Revenue Service
URL: http://www.irs.ustreas.gov/
IRS web site features their electronic publication, "The Digital Daily," with the latest news and forms from the IRS. Site also offers tax information, regulations, forms, publications and taxpayer help.

Library of Congress
URL: http://thomas.loc.gov/
Library of Congress information. Web site includes search feature to view major legislation, bill summaries, bill texts, Congressional Record texts, committee reports, historical documents and links to other U.S. Government Internet resources. Site includes profiles of Members of Congress and a detailed description of the legislative process.

Occupational Safety and Health Administration
URL: http://www.osha.gov/
OSHA's web site offers information on OSHA programs and services, media releases, standards, publications, statistics and data, OSHA documents and compliance assistance.

Patent and Trademark Office
URL: http://www.uspto.gov/
PTO web site offers ability to search patents, download forms, order copies, and offers information on fees and other legal materials.

Securities and Exchange Commission
URL: http://www.sec.gov/
SEC web site features information on the SEC, current news, investor assistance and complaints, EDGAR Database, SEC digests and statements, small business information, enforcement actions and current SEC rulemaking.

Small Business Administration
URL: http://www.sba.gov/
SBA web site offers information on starting, financing and/or expanding your business. Site also features the latest SBA news, the Small Business Act and regulations, and resources available by state and region.

Social Security Administration
URL: http://www.ssa.gov/
A fully searchable site on the topic of Social Security. Site includes information on benefits, publications, facts and figures, laws and regulations, public information resources, related sites, Supreme Court rulings, and recent legislation affecting benefits. View in both English or Spanish.

United States Customs Service
URL: http://www.ustreas.gov/treasury/bureaus/customs/customs.html
Web site features information on the Customs Service, the Customs electronic bulletin board (BBS), and Customs public auctions of seized property and other merchandise.

United States House of Representatives
URL: http://www.house.gov/
The official web site of the House of Representatives. Displays up to the hour committee hearing schedules, an annual Congressional schedule, a What's New feature, a House directory, extensive information on current bills and resolutions, and a searchable copy of the US Code. Site also contains a search feature for bills, committee reports, Congressional Records and links to other law resources on the web.

United States Postal Service
URL: http://www.usps.gov/
USPS web site allows you to look up ZIP+4 codes, track express mail, look up postal rates and products, notify the USPS of a change of address and other useful consumer information. Site also features Unforgettable Letters, InkCredible Stories and much more.

United States Senate
URL: http://www.senate.gov/
The official web site of the Senate. Site contains information on recent legislative actions, activities, and records. Features committee information and links to committee pages, a keyword search, profiles of Senators, Senate facts/statistics, and up-to-date developments.

The White House
URL: http://www.whitehouse.gov/
The official web site of The White House. Site provides information on commonly requested federal services, a virtual library containing searchable documents and speeches, and a briefing room with today's releases and federal statistics. Site features the Interactive Citizens Handbook, a comprehensive guide to federal government information.

STATE GOVERNMENT

Almost every state has a web site with helpful state information. We recommend visiting the following site for a complete list:

Piper Resources
URL: http://www.piperinfo.com/
Piper site offers the "State and Local Government on the Net" page which features a frequently updated directory of links to government sponsored and controlled resources on the Internet.

Sample list of state government web sites

California
URL: http://www.ca.gov/
CA state web site features information on California history, travel and vacation, doing business, working, natural resources, emergency relief and all aspects of the California government.

Florida
URL: http://www.state.fl.us/
FL state web site offers information on Florida government services, government telephone numbers, job vacancies, state licensing and links to other state government sites.

New York
URL: http://www.state.ny.us/
NY state web site features information on the Governor, tourism, education, state development, associations and links to other state government sites.

Texas
URL: http://www.texas.gov/
TX web site features information about "Texas for Texans, Future Texans, and Visitors." Site provides information on traveling in Texas, working in Texas, doing business in and with Texas, the Texas government and laws and access to the Texas Electronic Library.

GOVERNMENT WATCHDOG GROUPS

Congress Watch
URL: http://www.citizen.org/
An arm of Public Citizen, Congress Watch works for consumer-related legislation, regulation and policies in such areas as trade, health and safety and campaign financing and has publications available on the issues with which it deals.

Common Cause
URL: http://www.commoncause.org/
Common Cause is a nonprofit, nonpartisan citizens' lobby that concerns itself with campaign finance reform issues and the promotion of ethical standards and accountability in government.

HELP RESOLVING CONSUMER COMPLAINTS & CREDIT PROBLEMS

Each and every one of us is a consumer. Every day we purchase goods and services, everything from vacuum cleaners and computer equipment to chewing gum and newspapers. We also buy services—homebuilding, plumbing, auto repair and dry-cleaning, to name a few. Thanks to years of citizen activism, a system is now in place to protect us when something goes wrong in the marketplace. This chapter tells where you can turn to resolve consumer disputes and credit problems.

Unfortunately, not all merchants are ethical, honest, or mistake-free. Even if you shop wisely, making informed and rational buying decisions, you may still end up with subpar products and services. The last thing you want to have to do is take formal action to enforce your rights. If you have trouble with something you bought, you can and should take the following steps before contacting the offices listed in this chapter.

• Contact the person or business that sold you the item or service. Try to resolve the problem informally over the telephone; be sure to keep notes of whom you spoke with, the date of your conversation, and what, if anything, was promised.

• If your initial call gets no satisfactory result, call back and ask to speak to the supervisor of the one you spoke with on the first call. Continue this up the chain of command to the owner, president or chief executive officer, if necessary.

• Write a letter to the chief operating officer of the company, with copies to the public relations and customer service offices, reiterating the problem, identifying whom you spoke with, and explaining what remedy you're seeking and when you believe you should receive it. Remember to include copies of all supporting documents (i.e., sales receipts, warranties, bill of service).

At this point, the vast majority of consumer complaints are usually handled to the customer's satisfaction. For that small percentage of consumers who must continue to persist, write a second letter informing the company that you plan to file a formal complaint. You can contact one or more of the programs listed in this chapter for help identifying where such a complaint should be filed. Your options include Consumer Protection Offices (local or state government), Better Business Bureaus (private organizations), mass media consumer help-lines and, for those with credit problems, Credit Bureaus.

In the unlikely event that none of these options work, you still have the courtroom. For information on how to file a small claims suit, contact HALT for its book, *Small Claims Court: Making Your Way Through the System.*

CORPORATE HEADQUARTERS

This section lists the names and addresses of hundreds of corporate headquarters. If you have a complaint about a service or product, first try to resolve it with the seller. If that doesn't work, write or call the company's headquarters. Your letter of complaint should be addressed to the Customer Relations Department.

If you do not find the product name below, check the product label or warranty for the name and address of the manufacturer. Public libraries also have information that might be helpful. The Standard & Poor's Register of Corporations, Directors and Executives; Trade Names Directory; Standard Directory of Advertisers; and Dun & Bradstreet Directory are four sources that list information about most firms. If you cannot find the name of the manufacturer, the Thomas Register of American Manufacturers lists the manufacturers of thousands of products.

Remember, to save time, first take your complaint back to where you bought the product. If you contact the company's headquarters first, the consumer contact probably will direct you back to the local store where you made the purchase.

The following list is excerpted from the *1997 Consumer Resource Handbook,* published by the U.S. Office of Consumer Affairs.

A

AAMCO TRANSMISSIONS, INC.
1 Presidential Blvd.
Bala Cynwyd, PA 19004-1034
Phone: 610-668-2900
Toll free: 800-523-0401

AETNA LIFE AND CASUALTY
151 Farmington Ave.
Hartford, CT 06156
Phone: 203-273-0123
Toll free outside CT: 800-US-AETNA

AT&T
295 N. Maple Ave.
Basking Ridge, NJ 07920
Phone: 908-221-5311

ALAMO RENT-A-CAR
P.O. Box 22776
Ft. Lauderdale, FL 33335
Phone: 305-522-0000
Toll free: 800-445-5664

ALLIED VAN LINES
P.O. Box 4403
Chicago, IL 60680
Phone: 708-717-3590
Fax: 708-717-3123
Toll free: 800-470-2851

AMERICAN AIRLINES, INC.
P.O. Box 619612 MD 2400
DFW International Airport,
TX 75261-9612
Phone: 817-967-2000

AMERICAN EXPRESS CO.
777 American Express Way
Fort Lauderdale, FL 33337
Toll free: 800-528-4800
(Green Card inquiries)
Toll free: 800-327-2177
(Gold Card inquiries)
Toll free: 800-525-3355
(Platinum Card inquiries)

AMTRAK
Washington Union Station
60 Massachusetts Ave., N.E.
Washington, DC 20002
Phone: 202-906-2121
Toll free: 800-USA-RAIL
(reservations and information)

AMWAY CO.
7575 E. Fulton Rd.
Ada, MI 49355
Phone: 616-787-7717

ANDERSEN WINDOWS, INC.
100 Fourth Ave.
North Bayport, MN 55003
Phone: 612-430-5564

ANHEUSER-BUSCH, INC.
1 Busch Pl.
St. Louis, MO 63118-1852
Phone: 314-577-2000
Toll free: 800-342-5283
(consumer call center)

APPLE COMPUTER, INC.
20525 Mariani Ave.
Cupertino, CA 95014
Toll free: 800-776-2333
(complaints and questions)
Toll free: 800-538-9696
(dealer information)

B

BALI/SARA LEE INTIMATE
APPAREL SARA LEE CORPORATION
3330 Healy Dr.
P.O. Box 5100 (23113)
Winston-Salem, NC 27103
Toll free: 800-225-4872

BAYER CORP.
36 Columbia Rd.
Morristown, NJ 07962-1910
Toll free: 800-331-4536
(Sterling Health, Glenbrook, Winthrop
Consumer Products)

L.L. BEAN, INC.
Casco St.
Freeport, ME 04033-0001
Toll free: 800-341-4341

BEST WESTERN INTERNATIONAL
P.O. Box 42007
Phoenix, AZ 85080-2007
Toll free: 800-528-1238

BLACK AND DECKER
HOUSEHOLD PRODUCTS
6 Armstrong Rd.
Shelton, CT 06484
Toll free: 800-231-9786

BLACK AND DECKER
POWER TOOLS
626 Hanover Pike
Hampstead, MD 21074
Phone: 410-239-5300
Toll free: 800-762-6672

BLOCKBUSTER ENTERTAINMENT
1 Blockbuster Plaza
Ft. Lauderdale, FL 33301
Phone: 954-832-3000

**BLUE CROSS AND BLUE SHIELD
ASSOCIATION**
1310 G St., N.W., 12th Fl.
Washington, DC 20005
Phone: 202-626-4780
Fax: 202-626-4833

**BRADLEES DISCOUNT
DEPARTMENT STORES**
1 Bradlees Cir.
P.O. Box 9015
Braintree, MA 02184-9015
Phone: 617-380-5377

BRIDGESTONE/FIRESTONE, INC.
P.O. Box 7988
Chicago, IL 60680-9534
Toll free: 800-367-3872

BRISTOL-MYERS PRODUCTS
1350 Liberty Ave.
Hillside, NJ 07205
Toll free: 800-468-7746

**BRISTOL-MYERS SQUIBB
PHARMACEUTICAL GROUP**
P.O. Box 4000
Princeton, NJ 08543-4000
Phone: 609-252-4000
Toll free: 800-332-2056

BRITISH AIRWAYS
75-20 Astoria Blvd.
Jackson Heights, NY 11370
Phone: 718-397-4000

**BURLINGTON COAT FACTORY
WAREHOUSE CORP.**
1830 Route 130 North
Burlington, NJ 08016
Phone: 609-387-7800

C

CVS
1 CVS Dr.
Woonsocket, RI 02895-9988
Phone: 401-765-1500
Toll free: 800-555-4771
Fax: 401-762-6949

CAMPBELL SOUP CO.
Campbell Pl.
Camden, NJ 08103-1799
Phone: 609-342-3714
Toll free: 800-257-8443
Fax: 609-342-6449

CANON U.S.A., INC.
1 Canon Plaza, Bldg. C
Lake Success, NY 11042
Phone: 516-488-6700
Toll free: 800-828-4040

CIRCUIT CITY STORES, INC.
9950 Mayland Dr.
Richmond, VA 23233
Phone: 804-527-4000
Toll free: 800-627-2274

CLAIROL, INC.
300 Park Ave., South
New York, NY 10010
Voice/TDD Toll free: 800-223-5800
Voice/TDD Toll free: 800-HISPANA

CLOROX CO.
1221 Broadway
Oakland, CA 94612-1888
Phone: 510-271-7283
Toll free: 800-292-2200 (laundry brands)
Toll free: 800-537-2823 (food brands)
Toll free: 800-227-1860 (cleaners)
Toll free: 800-426-6228 (insecticides)
Toll free: 800-242-7482 (water systems)

THE COCA-COLA CO.
P.O. Drawer 1734
Atlanta, GA 30301
Toll free: 800-438-2653

COLDWELL BANKER CORP.
339 Jefferson Rd.
Parsippany, NJ 07054
Toll free: 800-733-6629

COLGATE, PALMOLIVE, MENNEN
300 Park Ave.
New York, NY 10022
Toll free: 800-228-7408

CRAFTMATIC ORGANIZATION
2500 Interplex Dr.
Trevose, PA 19053-6998
Phone: 215-639-1310
Toll free: 800-677-8200

JENNY CRAIG INTERNATIONAL
445 Marine View Ave.
Del Mar, CA 92014
Phone: 619-259-7000

CROWN BOOKS
3300 75th Ave.
Landover, MD 20785
Phone: 301-731-1200
Toll free: 800-831-7400

CUISINARTS CORP.
1 Cummings Point Rd.
Stamford, CT 06904
Phone: 203-975-4600
Phone: 609-426-1300 (in NJ)
Toll free outside NJ: 800-726-0190

D

DANNON CO., INC.
1111 Westchester Ave.
White Plains, NY 10604
(Written inquiries only)

DANSKIN
P.O. Box 15016
York, PA 17405-7016
Toll free: 800-288-6749

DEAN WITTER, DISCOVER & CO.
2 World Trade Ctr., 66th Fl.
New York, NY 10048
Toll free: 800-733-2307

DEERE & CO.
John Deere Rd.
Moline, IL 61265-8098
Phone: 309-765-8000

DEL MONTE FOODS
Consumer Affairs
P.O. Box 193575
San Francisco, CA 94119-3575
Toll free: 800-543-3090

DELTA AIR LINES
Hartsfield Atlanta International Airport
Atlanta, GA 30320
Phone: 404-715-1402

DELTA FAUCETS
P.O. Box 40980
Indianapolis, IN 46280
Phone: 317-848-1812

DENNY'S, INC.
203 E. Main St.
Spartanburg, SC 29319-0001
Phone: 864-597-8000

THE DIAL CORP.
15101 N. Scottsdale Rd.
Scottsdale, AZ 85254
Phone: 602-207-5518
Toll free: 800-528-0849 (foods division)
Toll free: 800-45-PUREX (laundry)
Toll free: 800-258-DIAL (personal care)

DOLE PACKAGED FOODS
5795 Lindero Canyon Rd.
Westlake Village, CA 91362-4013
Toll free: 800-232-8888

DOMINO'S PIZZA, INC.
P.O. Box 997
Ann Arbor, MI 48106-0997
Phone: 313-930-3030

DUNLOP TIRE CORP.
P.O. Box 1109
Buffalo, NY 14240-1109
Toll free: 800-548-4714

DUPONT CO.
BMP/Reeves Mill
Wilmington, DE 19880-0010
Toll free: 800-548-4714

**DURACELL USA DIVISION OF
DURACELL, INC.**
Duracell Dr.
Bethel, CT 06801
Phone: 203-796-4500
Toll free: 800-551-2355

E

EASTMAN KODAK CO.
343 State St.
Rochester, NY 14650-0811
Toll free: 800-242-2424

ELECTROLUX CORP.
2300 Windy Ridge Pkwy., Ste. 900
Marietta, GA 30067
Phone: 404-933-1000
Toll free: 800-243-9078

ENCYCLOPAEDIA BRITANNICA
310 S. Michigan Ave.
Chicago, IL 60604-4293
Phone: 312-347-7200

ESTEE LAUDER COMPANIES
767 Fifth Ave.
New York, NY 10153-0003
Phone: 212-572-4200

ETHAN ALLEN, INC.
Ethan Allen Dr.
Danbury, CT 06813
Phone: 203-743-8668
Fax: 203-743-8354
E-mail: ethanadv@ethanallen.com

THE EUREKA CO.
1201 E. Bell St.
Bloomington, IL 61701-6902
Phone: 309-823-5735
Toll free: 800-282-2886 (warranty)

BOB EVANS FARMS, INC.
3776 S. High St.
Columbus, OH 43207
Phone: 614-491-2225
Toll free outside OH: 800-272-7675
Fax: 614-492-4949

EXXON COMPANY U.S.A.
P.O. Box 2180
Houston, TX 77252-2180
Phone: 713-656-2111
Toll free: 800-243-9966
Fax: 713-656-9745

F

FAMILY CIRCLE MAGAZINE
110 Fifth Ave.
New York, NY 10011
Phone: 212-463-1124

FEDERAL EXPRESS CORP.
P.O Box 727, Dept. 1845
Memphis, TN 38194-1845
Phone: 901-395-4539
Toll free: 800-238-5355
Fax: 901-395-4511

FISHER PRICE
636 Girard Ave. East
Aurora, NY 14052
Toll free: 800-432-5437
Fax: 716-687-3494

**FLORIST TRANSWORLD
DELIVERY**
29200 Northwestern Hwy.
P.O. Box 2227
Southfield, MI 48037-4077
Phone: 810-355-9300
Toll free: 800-669-1000

FLORSHEIM SHOE CO.
130 S. Canal St.
Chicago, IL 60606-3999
Phone: 312-559-2549
Toll free: 800-633-4988

FORBES INC.
60 Fifth Ave.
New York, NY 10011
Phone: 212-620-2409
Fax: 212-620-5199

THE FRIGIDAIRE CO.
P.O. Box 7181
Dublin, OH 43017-0781
Toll free: 800-451-7007

FRUIT OF THE LOOM, INC.
1 Fruit of the Loom Dr.
Bowling Green, KY 42102-9015
Phone: 502-781-6400
Phone: 502-782-5400 (customer service)
Fax: 502-781-0903

FULLER BRUSH CO.
P.O. Box 1247
Great Bend, KS 67530-0729
Toll free: 800-523-3794
Fax: 316-793-4523

G

GTE CORP.
1 Stamford Forum
Stamford, CT 06904
Phone: 203-965-2000
Toll free: 800-548-2389

GENERAL MILLS, INC.
P.O. Box 1113
Minneapolis, MN 55440-1113
Phone: 612-540-4295
Toll free: 800-328-6787 (bakery)
Toll free: 800-328-1144 (cereals)
Toll free: 800-222-6846 (Gorton's)
Toll free: 800-231-0308 (snacks)

GENERAL MOTORS CORP.
2401 Columbus Ave., Mail Code 18-109
Anderson, IN 46016
Phone: 317-646-3000

**GENERAL MOTORS ACCEPTANCE
CORP. (GMAC)**
3044 W. Grand Blvd., Rm. AX348
Detroit, Ml 48202
Phone: 313-556-0510
Toll free: 800-441-9234

GENERAL TIRE INC.
1 General St.
Akron, OH 44329-0007
Toll free: 800-847-3349

GEORGIA-PACIFIC CORP.
P.O. Box 105605
Atlanta, GA 30348-5605
Phone: 404-652-4000
Phone: 770-953-7000

GERBER PRODUCTS CO.
445 State St.
Fremont, MI 49413-1056
Phone: 616-928-2000
Toll free: 800-4-GERBER (breast feeding)
Toll free: 800-828-9119 (baby formula)
Fax: 616-928-2723

GIANT FOOD INC.
P.O. Box 1804, Dept. 597
Washington, DC 20013
Phone: 301-341-4365
Fax: 301-618-4968

GILLETTE CO.
P.O. Box 61
Boston, MA 02199
Phone: 617-463-3337

GOODYEAR TIRE & RUBBER CO.
1144 E. Market St.
Akron, OH 44316
Phone: 330-796-3909
Fax Toll free: 800-321-2136

GREYHOUND LINES, INC.
P.O. Box 660362
Dallas, TX 75266-0362
Phone: 214-849-8000

H

H&R BLOCK, INC.
4410 Main St.
Kansas City, MO 64111-9986
Phone: 816-753-6900
Toll free: 800-829-7733

HALLMARK CARDS, INC.
P.O. Box 419034
Kansas City, MO 64141-6034
Toll free: 800-425-6275

HEINZ U.S.A.
P.O. Box 57
Pittsburgh, PA 15230
Phone: 412-237-5740
Fax: 412-237-5922

HERSHEY FOODS CORP.
100 Crystal A Dr.
Hershey PA 17033
Phone: 717-534-6799

HERTZ CORP.
225 Brae Blvd.
Park Ridge, NJ 07656-0713
Phone: 201-307-2000
Toll free: 800-654-3131 (reservations)
Fax: 201-307-2644

HEWLETT-PACKARD CO.
19310 Prune Ridge Ave.,
Mail Stop 49AU25
Cupertino, CA 95014-0604
Toll free: 800-752-0900
Fax: 408-345-8178

HIT OR MISS
100 Campanelli Pkwy.
Stoughton, MA 02072
Phone: 617-344-0800
Fax: 617-297-7268

HOME DEPOT INC.
2727 Paces Ferry Rd., NW
Atlanta, GA 30339
Phone: 404-433-8211
Toll free: 800-553-3199

HONEYWELL, INC.
Honeywell Plaza
P.O. Box 524
Minneapolis, MN 55440-0524
Phone: 612-951-1000
Toll free: 800-468-1502

HOOVER CO.
101 E. Maple North
Canton, OH 44720
Phone: 330-499-9499
Toll free: 800-944-9200

HORMEL FOODS CO.
1 Hormel Pl.
Austin, MN 55912-9989
Phone: 507-437-5940
Toll free: 800-523-4635

HUFFY BICYCLE CO.
P.O. Box 1204
Dayton, OH 45401
Phone: 513-866-6251
Toll free: 800-872-2453
Fax: 513-865-2835

I

**IBM INTERNATIONAL
SERVICES CTR.**
300 E. Valencia
Tucson, AZ 85706
Toll free: 800-426-3333

J

JVC COMPANY OF AMERICA
107 Little Falls Rd.
Fairfield, NJ 07004
Phone: 201-808-2100
Toll free: 800-252-5722
Fax: 201-808-3351

**JOHN HANCOCK FINANCIAL
SERVICES**
P.O. Box 111
Boston, MA 02117
Phone: 617-572-6272

JOHNNY APPLESEED'S, INC.
30 Tozer Rd.
Beverly, MA 01915
Toll free: 800-767-6666

**JOHNSON & JOHNSON
CONSUMER PRODUCTS, INC.**
199 Grandview Rd.
Skillman, NJ 08558
Phone: 908-874-1000

HOWARD JOHNSON, INC.
3400 N.W. Grand Ave.
Phoenix, AZ 85017
Phone: 602-264-9164

K

K-MART CORP.
3100 W. Big Beaver Rd.
Troy, MI 48084
Phone: 810-643-1643

KAWASAKI MOTOR CORP., U.S.A.
Consumer Services
P.O. Box 25252
Santa Ana, CA 92799-5252
Phone: 714-770-0400

KELLOGG CO.
P.O. Box CAMB
Battle Creek, MI 49016
Toll free: 800-962-1413

KIMBERLY-CLARK CORP.
P.O. Box 2020
Neenah, WI 54957-2020
Phone: 414-721-8000
Toll free: 800-544-1847

KITCHENAID
2000 M-63 North
Benton Harbor, MI 49022
Phone: 616-923-4500
Toll free: 800-422-1230

KRAFT, INC.
Kraft Court
Glenview, IL 60025
Toll free: 800-323-0768

KROGER CO.
1014 Vine St.
Cincinnati, OH 45202
Phone: 513-762-1589
Toll free: 800-632-6900

L

LA GEAR
2850 Ocean Park Blvd.
Santa Monica, CA 90405
Phone: 310-452-4327
Toll free: 800-786-7800

LA-Z-BOY CHAIR CO.
1284 N. Telegraph Rd.
Monroe, MI 48162-3309
Phone: 313-242-1444

LECHMERE
275 Wildwood St.
Woburn, MA 01801
Phone: 617-476-1404
Toll free: 800-733-4666

L'EGGS PRODUCTS
5660 University Pkwy.
Winston-Salem, NC 27105
Phone: 910-768-9540

LENNOX INDUSTRIES
P.O Box 799900
Dallas, TX 75379-9900
Phone: 214-497-5000

LEVI STRAUSS & CO.
1155 Battery St.
San Francisco, CA 94111
Toll free: 800-USA-LEVI

LEVITZ FURNITURE CORP.
6111 Broken Sound Pkwy., NW
Boca Raton, FL 33487-2799
Toll free: 800-631-4601

LILLIAN VERNON CORP.
2600 International Pkwy.
Virginia Beach, VA 23452
Phone: 804-430-1500
Toll free: 800-285-5555

ELI LILLY & CO.
Lilly Corporate Ctr.
Indianapolis, IN 46285
Phone: 317-276-8588

THE LIMITED, INC.
Three Limited Pkwy.
Columbus, OH 43230
Phone: 614-479-7000

LONG JOHN SILVER'S
315 S. Broadden
Lexington, KY 40508
Phone: 606-388-6000

LOS ANGELES TIMES
Times Mirror Square
Los Angeles, CA 90053
Phone: 213-237-5000

M

MCI COMMUNICATIONS
1200 S. Hayes St., 11th Fl.
Arlington, VA 22202
Toll free: 800-677-6580

M&M/MARS, INC.
High St.
Hacketstown, NJ 07840
Phone: 908-852-1000

MARRIOTT CORP.
1 Marriott Dr.
Washington, DC 20058
Phone: 301-380-3000

MASTERCARD INTERNATIONAL
(contact issuing bank)
Toll free: 800-826-2181 (lost or stolen
cards or questions about the MasterCard
system)

MATTEL TOYS, INC.
333 Continental Blvd.
El Segundo, CA 90245-5012
Phone: 310-252-2000
Toll free: 800-524-TOYS

MAY DEPARTMENT STORES
611 Olive St.
St. Louis, MO 63101
Phone: 314-342-6300

MCDONALD'S CORP.
Kroc Dr.
Oak Brook, IL 60521
Phone: 708-575-6198

MEINEKE DISCOUNT MUFFLER
128 S. Tryon St., Ste. 900
Charlotte, NC 28202
Phone: 704-377-3070

MERCK
100 Summit Ave.
Montvale, NJ 07645
Phone: 201-358-5530
Fax: 201-358-5793

**MERRILL LYNCH PIERCE
FENNER & SMITH**
265 Davidson Ave., 4th Fl.
Somerset, NJ 08873
Phone: 908-563-8777

MICHELIN TIRE CORP.
P.O. Box 19001
Greenville, SC 29602
Toll free: 800-847-3435

MILTON BRADLEY CO.
443 Shaker Rd., East
Long Meadow, MA 01028
Phone: 413-525-6411, ext. 2288
Fax: 413-525-1767

MINOLTA CORP.
101 Williams Dr.
Ramsey, NJ 07446
Phone: 201-825-4000
Fax: 201-825-7605

MOBIL OIL CORP.
3225 Gallows Rd.
Fairfax, VA 22037
Toll free: 800-662-4592

MONTGOMERY WARD
1 Montgomery Ward Plaza, 9-S
Chicago, IL 60671
Toll free: 800-695-3553

**MUTUAL OF OMAHA
INSURANCE CO.**
Mutual of Omaha Plaza
Omaha, NE 68175
Phone: 402-342-7600
Fax: 402-351-2775

N

NBC
30 Rockefeller Plaza
New York, NY 10112
Phone: 212-664-2333

NABISCO FOODS GROUP
100 DeForest Ave.
East Hanover, NJ 07936
Phone: 201-503-2617
Toll free: 800-NABISCO
Fax: 201-503-2202

NEAR EAST FOOD PRODUCTS
797 Lancaster St.
Leominster, MA 01453
Toll free: 800-822-7423

NEIMAN-MARCUS
P.O. Box 729080
Dallas, TX 75372
Toll free: 800-685-6695
Fax: 214-761-2650

NESTLÉ USA, INC.
P.O. Box 29055
Glendale, CA 91209-9055

NIKE, INC.
Nike/World Campus
1 Bowerman Dr.
Beaverton, OR 97005
Toll free: 800-344-6453

NINE WEST GROUP
Corporate Headquarters
9 W. Broad St.
Stamford, CT 06902
Phone: 203-324-7567

NUTRI/SYSTEM INC.
410 Horsham Rd.
Horsham, PA 10944
Phone: 215-445-5300

O

OCEAN SPRAY CRANBERRIES INC.
1 Ocean Spray Dr.
Lakeville/Middleboro, MA 02349
Phone: 508-946-7407
Toll free: 800-662-3263
Fax: 508-946-7720

OLAN MILLS, INC.
4325 Amnicola Hwy.
P.O. Box 23456
Chattanooga TN 37422-3456
Phone: 615-622-5141
Toll free: 800-251-6323
Fax: 615-499-3864

ORE-IDA FOODS, INC.
P.O. Box 10
Boise, ID 83707
Toll free: 800-842-2401

OWENS CORNING
World Headquarters
Fiberglas Tower
Toledo, OH 43659-0001
Phone: 419-248-8000

P

PACIFIC BELL
140 New Montgomery St.
San Francisco, CA 94105
Toll free in CA: 800-791-6661
Toll free outside CA: 800-697-6547

PAINEWEBBER INC.
1000 Harbor Blvd., 8th Fl.
Weehawken, NJ 07087
Phone: 201-902-4936
Toll free: 800-354-9103
Fax: 201-902-5795

J.C. PENNEY CO., INC.
P.O. Box 10001
Dallas, TX 75301-8212
Phone: 214-431-8500
Fax: 214-431-8792

PEPPERIDGE FARM, INC.
595 Westport Ave.
Norwalk, CT 06851
Phone: 203-846-7276
Fax: 203-846-7278

PEPSI-COLA CO.
1 Pepsi Way
Somers, NY 10589-2201
Toll free: 800-433-2652
Fax: 914-767-7761

PERDUE FARMS
P.O. Box 1537
Salisbury, MD 21802
Phone: 410-543-3000
Toll free outside MD: 800-442-2034
Fax: 410-543-3292

THE PERRIER GROUP
777 West Putnam Ave.
Greenwich, CT 06830
Phone: 203-531-4100
Fax: 203-863-0256

PET INC.
P.O. Box 66719
St. Louis, MO 63166-6719
Phone: 314-622-6695
Toll free: 800-325-7130

PHARMACIA AND UPJOHN CORP.
Consumer Products Division
Patient Information (prescriptions)
7000 Portage Rd.
Kalamazoo, MI 49001
Toll free: 800-253-8600

PHILIP MORRIS COMPANIES, INC.
120 Park Ave.
New York, NY 10017
Phone: 212-880-3366
Toll free: 800-343-0975

PILLSBURY CO.
Consumer Response
P.O. Box 550
Minneapolis, MN 55440
Toll free: 800-767-4466

PLAYSKOOL CONSUMER AFFAIRS
P.O. Box 200
Pawtucket, RI 02862-0200
Toll free: 800-752-9755
Fax: 401-431-8464

POLAROID CORP.
1 Burlington Rd.
Bedford, MA 01730
Phone: 617-386-2000 (collect calls
accepted within MA)
Toll free outside MA: 800-343-5000
Fax: 617-386-5605

PROCTER & GAMBLE CO.
P.O. Box 599
Cincinnati, OH 45201-0599
Phone: 513-945-8787
(Toll free numbers appear on all Procter & Gamble product labels)

PUBLISHERS CLEARING HOUSE
382 Channel Dr.
Port Washington, NY 11050
Phone: 516-883-5432
Toll free: 800-645-9242
Fax: 800-453-0272

Q

QUAKER OATS CO.
Consumer Response
P.O. Box 049003
Chicago, IL 60604-9003
Check product package for toll-free number or call: 312-222-7111

R

READERS DIGEST ASSOCIATION
Pleasantville, NY 10570-7000
Toll free: 800-431-1246
Fax: 914-238-4559

REEBOK INTERNATIONAL, LTD.
100 Technology Ctr. Dr.
Stoughton, MA 02072
Toll free: 800-843-4444

REMINGTON PRODUCTS CO.
60 Main St.
Bridgeport, CT 06004
Phone: 203-367-4400
Toll free: 800-736-4648

ROCKPORT
220 Donald Lynch Blvd.
Marlboro, MA 01752
Toll free: 800-343-9255
Fax: 508-624-4299

ROLEX WATCH U.S.A. INC.
665 Fifth Ave.
New York, NY 10022
Phone: 212-758-7700
Fax: 212-980-2166

ROSS LABORATORIES
625 Cleveland Ave.
Columbus, OH 43215
Phone: 614-624-7900
Toll free: 800-227-5767
Fax: 614-624-7919

RUBBERMAID, INC.
1147 Akron Rd.
Wooster, OH 44691-0800
Phone: 330-264-6464, ext. 2619
Fax: 330-287-2751

RYDER TRUCK RENTAL
P.O. Box 020816
Miami, FL 33102-0816
Toll free: 800-327-7777
Fax: 305-593-4463

S

SAFEWAY INC.
Oakland, CA 94660
Phone: 510-891-3267

SARA LEE CORP.
Three First National Plaza
70 W. Madison St.
Chicago, IL 60602-4260
Phone: 312-726-2600
Toll free: 800-621-5235
Fax: 312-726-3712

SEALY MATTRESS
1228 Euclid Ave., 10th Fl.
Cleveland, OH 44115
Phone: 216-522-1310
Fax: 216-522-1366

SERTA, INC.
325 Spring Lake Dr.
Itasca, IL 60143
Phone: 708-285-9300
Toll free: 800-426-0371
Fax: 708-285-9330

SHELL OIL CO.
Box 4650
Houston, TX 77252
Toll free: 800-248-4257

SHERWIN-WILLIAMS
Group 101 Prospect Ave., NW
Cleveland, OH 44115-1075
Phone: 216-566-2151

SIMMONS CO.
6424 Warren Dr.
P.O. Box 2768
Norcross GA 30093
Toll free: 800-654-9258

SINGER SEWING CO.
P.O. Box 1909
Edison, NJ 08818-1909
Phone: 908-225-8844
Toll free: 800-877-7762

SLIM FAST FOODS CO.
777 S. Flager Dr., West Tower, Ste. 1400
West Palm Beach, FL 33401
Toll free: 800-223-1248

SNAPPLE BEVERAGES
Consumer Response Ctr.
333 W. Merrick Rd.
Valley Stream, NY 11580
Toll Free: 800-Snapple (762-7753)

SONY CORP. OF AMERICA
Sony Service Co.
1 Sony Dr.
Park Ridge, NJ 07656
Toll free: 800-282-2848

SOUTHWEST AIRLINES
Love Field
P.O. Box 36611
Dallas, TX 75235-1611
Phone: 214-904-4223

SPRINT
1603 LBJ Freeway, Ste. 300
Dallas, TX 75234
Toll free: 800-347-8988
Fax: 214-405-6114

STOP & SHOP
P.O. Box 1942
Boston, MA 02105
Phone: 617-770-6040

T

3M
3M Ctr., Bldg. 225-5N-04
St. Paul, MN 55144-1000
Phone: 612-733-1871
Toll free: 800-364-3577
Fax: 612-736-3094

TRW INFORMATION SERVICES
P.O. Box 949
Allen, TX 75002-0949
Phone: 214-235-1200

TANDY CORP./ RADIO SHACK
600 1 Tandy Ctr.
Fort Worth, TX 76102
Phone: 817-390-3218
Fax: 817-390-3292

TARGET STORES
33 South 6th St.
P.O. Box 1392
Minneapolis, MN 55440-1392
Phone: 612-304-4996

TEXACO
P.O. Box 790001
Houston, TX 77094
Phone: 713-647-1500

TEXAS INSTRUMENTS, INC.
P.O. Box 6118
Temple, TX 76503-6118
Phone: 817-774-6827
Toll free: 800-842-2737
Fax: 817-774-6074

THOM MCANN SHOE CO.
67 Millbrook St.
Worcester, MA 01606-2804
Phone: 508-791-3811
Fax: 508-792-2908

TIMEX CORP.
P.O. Box 2740
Little Rock, AR 72203-2740
Phone: 501-372-1111
Toll free: 800-448-4639
Fax: 570-370-5747

TONKA PRODUCTS
P.O. Box 200
Pawtucket, RI 02861-0200
Toll free: 800-248-6652

THE TORO CO.
8111 Lyndale Ave., South
Minneapolis, MN 55420
Phone: 612-887-8900

TOYS "R" US
461 From Rd.
Paramus, NJ 07652
Phone: 201-599-7897
Fax: 201-262-8919

TRAK AUTO
3300 75th Ave.
Landover, MD 20785
Phone: 301-731-1200
Toll free: 800-835-7300
Fax: 301-731-1470

TRANS WORLD AIRLINES, INC.
110 S. Bedford Rd.
Mt. Kisco, NY 10549
Phone: 314-589-3600
Fax: 314-589-3626

TUPPERWARE
P.O. Box 2353
Orlando, FL 32802-2353
Toll free: 800-858-7221
Fax: 407-847-1897

TYSON FOODS
P.O. Box 2020
Springdale, AR 72765-2020
Phone: 501-290-4714
Toll free: 800-233-6332
Fax: 501-290-7930

U

U-HAUL INTERNATIONAL
Phoenix, AZ 85036-1120
Toll free: 800-528-0463
Fax: 602-263-6984

UNIROYAL GOODRICH TIRE CO.
P.O. Box 19001
Greenville, SC 29602-9001
Toll free: 800-521-9796
Fax: 864 458-6650

UNITED AIRLINES
P.O. Box 66100
Chicago, IL 60666
Phone: 847-700-6796
Toll free: 800-323-0710

UNITED PARCEL SERVICE
55 Glenlake Pkwy.
Atlanta, GA 30328
Phone: 404-828-6000

**UNITED STATES FIDELITY &
GUARANTEE CO. (USF&G)**
100 Light St.
Baltimore, MD 21202
Phone: 410-547-3000

UNITED VAN LINES, INC.
1 United Dr.
Fenton, MO 63026
Toll free: 800-325-9980
Toll free: 800-325-9970 (claims)

US AIRWAYS
P.O. Box 1501
Winston-Salem, NC 27102-1501
Phone: 910-661-0061
Fax: 910-661-8187

V

VAN HEUSEN CO.
1001 Frontier Rd.
Bridgewater, NJ 08807
Phone: 908-685-0050

VISA USA, INC.
P.O. Box 8999
San Francisco, CA 94128-8999
Phone: 415-432-3200
Fax: 415-432-4153
(Cardholders should always call issuing
bank first.)

W

WALGREEN CO.
200 Wilmot Rd.
Deerfield, IL 60015
Phone: 847-940-2500
Toll free: 800-289-2273

WAL-MART STORES, INC.
702 S.W. Eighth St.
Bentonville, AR 72716-0117
Phone: 501-273-4000

WEIGHT WATCHERS FOOD
P.O. Box 10
Boise, ID 83707
Toll free: 800-651-6000

WENDY'S INTERNATIONAL, INC.
P.O Box 256
Dublin, OH 43017-0256
Phone: 614-764-6800

**WESTERN UNION FINANCIAL
SERVICES, INC.**
13022 Hollenberg Dr.
Bridgeton, MO 63044
Phone: 314-291-8000

WHIRLPOOL CORP.
2303 Pipestone Rd.
Benton Harbor, MI 49022-2427

WILLIAMS-SONOMA
100 N. Point St.
San Francisco, CA 94133
Toll free: 800-541-1262

F.W. WOOLWORTH CO.
233 Broadway
New York, NY 10279-0001
Phone: 212-553-2000

X

XEROX CORP.
100 Clinton Ave., South
Rochester, NY 14644
Phone: 716-423-5490

Y

YAMAHA MOTOR CORP.
6555 Katella Ave.
Cypress, CA 90630-5101
Phone: 714-761-7439
Fax: 714-761-7559

Z

ZALE CORP.
901 W. Walnut Hill Ln.
Irving, TX 75038-1003
Phone: 214-580-5104
Fax: 214-580-5523

ZENITH ELECTRONICS CORP.
1000 Milwaukee Ave.
Glenview, IL 60025-2493
Phone: 847-391-8100
Toll free: 800-488-8129

ZENITH PACKARD BELL
8285 West 3500 South
Magna, UT 84044
Toll free: 800-227-3360
Fax: 708-808-4468

CONSUMER PROTECTION OFFICES

Consumer Protection Agencies resolve individual complaints against businesses and educate consumers and businesses about the law. They also provide information about consumer complaints filed against businesses in their area of jurisdiction. Some are operated by the state government, other by local governments.

To file a complaint, call the nearest offices listed below and ask if your complaint needs to be in writing and on a particular form or if you can report it over the telephone. Some offices may ask you to come in for an interview. State offices may refer you to a local or county office.

The list of consumer protection offices is excerpted from the *1997 Consumer Resource Handbook,* published by the U.S. Office of Consumer Affairs.

ALABAMA

State Office:
Dennis Wright, Chief Director
Consumer Affairs Division
Office of Attorney General
11 S. Union St.
Montgomery, AL 36130
Phone: 334-242-7334
Toll free in AL: 800-392-5658
Fax: 334-242-2433

ALASKA

The Consumer Protection Section in the Office of the Attorney General has been closed. Consumers with complaints are being referred to the Better Business Bureau (see page 105), small claims court and private attorneys.

ARIZONA

State Offices:
Sydney K. Davis, Chief Counsel
Consumer Protection
Office of the Attorney General
1275 W. Washington St., Rm. 259
Phoenix, AZ 85007
Phone: 602-542-3702
Phone: 602-542-5763
Toll free in AZ: 800-352-8431
Fax: 602-542-4377
TDD: 602-542-5002

Noreen Matts
Assistant Attorney General
Consumer Protection
Office of the Attorney General
400 W. Congress South Bldg., Ste. 315
Tucson, AZ 85701
Phone: 602-628-6504

ARKANSAS

State Office:
Kay Dewitt, Director
Consumer Protection Division
Office of Attorney General
200 Catlett Prien
323 Center St.
Little Rock, AR 72201
Phone: 501-682-2341
Voice/TDD in AR: 800-482-8982
TDD: 501-682-2014

CALIFORNIA

State Offices:
Marjorie Berte, Director
California Dept. of Consumer Affairs
400 R St., Ste. 3000
Sacramento, CA 95814
Phone: 916-445-4465
Toll free in CA: 800-952-5200
TDD: 916-322-1700

Office of Attorney General
Public Inquiry Unit
P.O. Box 944255
Sacramento, CA 94244-2550
Phone: 916-322-3360
Toll free in CA: 800-952-5225
TDD: 916-324-5564

Marty Keller, Chief
Bureau of Automotive Repair
California Dept. of Consumer Affairs
10240 Systems Pky.
Sacramento, CA 95827
Phone: 916-445-1254
Toll free in CA: 800-952-5210
(auto repair only)
TDD: 916-322-1700

COLORADO

State Office:
Consumer Protection Unit
Office of Attorney General
1525 Sherman St., 5th Fl.
Denver, CO 80203-1760
Phone: 303-866-5189

CONNECTICUT

State Offices:
Mark A. Shiffrin, Commissioner
Department of Consumer Protection
165 Capitol Ave.
Hartford, CT 06106
Phone: 860-566-2534
Toll free in CT: 800-842-2649
Fax: 860-566-1531

Steven M. Rutstein
Assistant Attorney General
Antitrust/Consumer Protection
Office of Attorney General
110 Sherman St.
Hartford, CT 06105
Phone: 860-566-5374
Fax: 860-523-5536

DELAWARE

State Offices:
Mary McDonough, Director
Consumer Protection Unit
Department of Justice
820 N. French St.
Wilmington, DE 19801
Phone: 302-577-3250
Fax: 302-577-6499

Eugene M. Hall,
Deputy Attorney General
Fraud and Consumer Protection Unit
Office of Attorney General
820 N. French St.
Wilmington, DE 19801
Phone: 302-577-2500
Fax: 302-577-6499

DISTRICT OF COLUMBIA

Hampton Cross, Director
Department of Consumer and
Regulatory Affairs
614 H St., NW
Washington, DC 20001
Phone: 202-727-7120
Fax: 202-727-8073
Fax: 202-727-7842

FLORIDA

State Offices:
James P. Kelly, Director
Department of Agriculture and
Consumer Services
Division of Consumer Services
407 S. Calhoun St., Mayo Bldg., 2nd Fl.
Tallahassee, FL 32399-0800
Phone: 904-488-2221
Toll free in FL: 800-435-7352
Fax: 904-487-4177

Jack A. Norris, Jr., Chief
Consumer Litigation Section
110 S.E. 6th St.
Fort Lauderdale, FL 33301
Phone: 954-712-4600
Fax: 954-712-4706

Cecile Dykas
Assistant Deputy Attorney General
Economic Crimes Division
Office of Attorney General
110 S.E. 6th St.
Fort Lauderdale, FL 33301
Phone: 954-712-4600
Fax: 954-712-4658

GEORGIA

State Office:
Barry W. Reid, Administrator
Governor's Office of Consumer Affairs
2 Martin Luther King, Jr. Dr., SE,
Ste. 356
Atlanta, GA 30334
Phone: 404-656-3790
Toll free in GA: 800-869-1123
Fax: 404-651-9018

HAWAII

State Offices:
JoAnn M. Uchida, Executive Director
Office of Consumer Protection
Department of Commerce and
Consumer Affairs
235 S. Beretania St., Rm. 801
P.O. Box 3767
Honolulu, HI 96813-3767
Phone: 808-586-2636
Fax: 808-586-2640

Gene Murayama, Investigator
Office of Consumer Protection
Department of Commerce and
 Consumer Affairs
75 Aupuni St.
Hilo, HI 96720
Phone: 808-974-6230

Janice Borngraber, Investigator
Office of Consumer Protection
Department of Commerce and
Consumer Affairs
54 High St.
P.O. Box 1098
Wailuku, HI 96793
Phone: 808-984-8244

IDAHO

State Office:
Brett De Lange, Deputy Attorney General
Office of the Attorney General
Consumer Protection Unit
650 W. State St.
Boise, ID 83720-0010
Phone: 208-334-2424
Toll free in ID: 800-432-3545
Fax: 208-334-2830

ILLINOIS

State Offices:
Jim Ryan, Attorney General
Governors Office of Citizens Assistance
222 S. College
Springfield, IL 62706
Phone: 217-782-0244
Toll free in IL: 800-642-3112
(handles problems related to state
government)

Patricia Kelly, Chief
Consumer Protection Division
Office of Attorney General
100 W. Randolph, 12th Fl.
Chicago, IL 60601
Phone: 312-814-3000
TDD: 312-793-2852

Charles Gil Fergus, Bureau Chief
Consumer Fraud Bureau
100 W. Randolph, 13th Fl.
Chicago, IL 60601
Phone: 312-814-3580
Toll free in IL: 800-386-5438
TDD: 312-814-3374

INDIANA

State Office:
Lisa Hayes
Chief Counsel and Director
Consumer Protection Division
Office of Attorney General
Indiana Government Center South, 5th Fl.
402 W. Washington St.
Indianapolis, IN 46204
Phone: 317-232-6330
Toll free in IN: 800-382-5516

IOWA

State Office:
William Branch
Assistant Attorney General
Consumer Protection Division
Office of Attorney General
1300 E. Walnut St., 2nd Fl.
Des Moines, IA 50319
Phone: 515-281-5926
Fax: 515-281-6771

KANSAS

State Office:
C. Steven Rarrick
Deputy Attorney General
Consumer Protection Division
Office of Attorney General
301 W. 10th
Kansas Judicial Center
Topeka, KS 66612-1597
Phone: 913-296-3751
Toll free in KS: 800-432-2310
Fax: 913-291-3699

KENTUCKY

State Offices:
Todd Leatherman, Director
Consumer Protection Division
Office of Attorney General
1024 Capital Center Dr.
P.O. Box 2000
Frankfort, KY 40601-2000
Phone: 502-573-2200

Robert L. Winlock, Administrator
Consumer Protection Division
Office of Attorney General
107 S. 4th St.
Louisville, KY 40202
Phone: 502-595-3262
Fax: 502-595-4627

LOUISIANA

State Office:
Tamera R. Velasquez, Chief
Consumer Protection Section
Office of Attorney General
1 America Place
P.O. Box 94095
Baton Rouge, LA 70804-9095
Phone: 504-342-9638
Fax: 504-342-9637

MAINE

State Offices:
William N. Lund, Director
Office of Consumer Credit Regulation
State House Station
Augusta, ME 04333-0035
Phone: 207-624-8527
Toll free in ME: 800-332-8529
Fax: 207-582-7699

Stephen Wessler, Chief
Consumer and Antitrust Division
Office of Attorney General
State House Station No. 6
Augusta, ME 04333
Phone: 207-626-8849

MARYLAND

State Offices:
William Leibovici, Chief
Consumer Protection Division
Office of Attorney General
200 St. Paul Pl., 16th Fl.
Baltimore, MD 21202-2021
Phone: 410-528-8662 (consumer hotline)
Fax: 410-576-6566
TDD: 410-576-6372 (Baltimore area)

Jack Joyce, Director
Licensing & Consumer Services
Motor Vehicle Administration
6601 Ritchie Hwy., NE
Glen Burnie, MD 21062
Phone: 410-768-7535
Fax: 410-768-7167

Emalu Myer
Consumer Affairs Specialist
Eastern Shore Branch Office
Consumer Protection Division
Office of Attorney General
201 Baptist St., Ste. 30
Salisbury, MD 21801-4976
Phone: 410-543-6642

Larry Munson, Director
Western Maryland Branch Office
Consumer Protection Division
Office of Attorney General
138 E. Antietam St., Ste. 210
Hagerstown, MD 21740-5684
Phone: 301-791-4780

MASSACHUSETTS

State Offices:
George Weber, Chief
Consumer and Antitrust Division
Department of Attorney General
1 Ashburton Pl.
Boston, MA 02108
Phone: 617-727-2200
(information and referral to local consumer offices that work in conjunction with the Department of Attorney General)
Fax: 617-727-5765

Priscilla H. Douglas, Secretary
Executive Office of Consumer Affairs
and Business Regulation
One Ashburton Pl., Rm. 1411
Boston, MA 02108
Phone: 617-727-7780 (information and referral only)
Fax: 617-227-6094

Thomas J. McCormick
Assistant Attorney General
Western Massachusetts Consumer
Protection Division
Department of Attorney General
436 Dwight St.
Springfield, MA 01103
Phone: 413-784-1240
Fax: 413-784-1244

MICHIGAN

State Offices:
Frederick H. Hoffecker
Assistant in Charge
Consumer Protection Division
Office of Attorney General
P.O. Box 30213
Lansing, MI 48909
Phone: 517-373-1140
Fax: 517-335-1935

Rodger James, Director
Bureau of Automotive Regulation
Michigan Department of State
Lansing, MI 48918-1200
Phone: 517-373-4777
Toll free in MI: 800-292-4204
Fax: 517-373-0964

MINNESOTA

State Office:
Curt Loewe, Director
Consumer Services Division
Office of Attorney General
1400 NCL Tower
445 Minnesota St.
St. Paul, MN 55101
Phone: 612-296-3353

MISSISSIPPI

State Offices:
Leyser Q. Morris
Special Assistant Attorney General
Director, Office of Consumer Protection
P.O. Box 22947
Jackson, MS 39225-2947
Phone: 601-359-4230
Fax: 601-359-4231
Toll free in MS: 800-281-4418

Joe B. Hardy, Director
Bureau of Regulatory Services
Department of Agriculture & Commerce
121 N. Jefferson St.
P.O. Box 1609
Jackson, MS 39201
Phone: 601-354-7063

MISSOURI

State Office:
Doug Ommen, Chief Counsel
Consumer Protection Division
Office of Attorney General
P.O. Box 899
Jefferson City, MO 65102
Phone: 573-751-3321
Toll free in MO: 800-392-8222
Fax: 314-751-7948

MONTANA

State Office:
Annie Bartos, Chief Legal Counsel
Consumer Affairs Unit
Department of Commerce
1424 9th Ave.
Box 200501
Helena, MT 59620-0501
Phone: 406-444-4312
Fax: 406-444-2903

NEBRASKA

State Office:
Paul N. Potadle
Assistant Attorney General
Consumer Protection Division
Department of Justice
2115 State Capitol
P.O. Box 98920
Lincoln, NE 68509
Phone: 402-471-2682
Fax: 402-471 3297

NEVADA

State Offices:
Patricia Morse Jarman
Commissioner of Consumer Affairs
Department of Business and Industry
1850 E. Sahara, Ste. 101
Las Vegas, NV 89158
Phone: 702-486-7355
Toll free in NV: 800-326-5202
Fax: 702-486-7371
TDD: 702-486-7901

Ray Trease,
Supervisory Compliance Investigator
Consumer Affairs Division
Department of Business and Industry
4600 Kietzke Ln., B-113
Reno, NV 89502
Phone: 702-688-1800
Toll free in NV: 800-326-5202
Fax: 702-688-1803
TDD: 702-486-7901

NEW HAMPSHIRE

State Office:
Chief
Consumer Protection
and Antitrust Bureau
Office of Attorney General
33 Capitol St.
Concord, NH 03301
Phone: 603-271-3641
Fax: 603-271-2110

NEW JERSEY

State Offices:
Mark S. Herr, Director
Division of Consumer Affairs
P.O. Box 45027
Newark, NJ 07101
Phone: 201-504-6534
Fax: 201-648-3538

Lauren F. Carlton
Deputy Attorney General
New Jersey Division of Law
P.O. Box 45029
124 Halsey St., 5th Fl.
Newark, NJ 07101
Phone: 201-648-7579
Fax: 201-648-3879

NEW MEXICO

State Office:
Consumer Protection Division
Office of Attorney General
P.O. Drawer 1508
Santa Fe, NM 87504
Phone: 505-827-6060
Toll free in NM: 800-678-1508

NEW YORK

State Offices:
Susan Somers, Deputy Chief
Bureau of Consumer Frauds
and Protection
Office of Attorney General
State Capitol
Albany, NY 12224
Phone: 518-474-5481
Toll free: 800-771-7755 (hotline)
Fax: 518-474-3618

Timothy S. Carey
Chairman and Executive Director
Consumer Protection Board
5 Empire State Plaza, Ste. 2101
Albany, NY 12223-1556
Phone: 518-474-8583
Fax: 518-474-2474

Shirley Sarna
Assistant Attorney General in Charge
Bureau of Consumer Frauds
and Protection
Office of Attorney General
120 Broadway
New York, NY 10271
Phone: 212-416-8345
Toll free: 800-771-7755
TDD: 212-416-8940

NORTH CAROLINA

State Office:
Alan S. Hirsch
Special Deputy Attorney General
Consumer Protection Section
Office of Attorney General
Raney Bldg.
P.O. Box 629
Raleigh, NC 27602
Phone: 919-733-7741
Fax: 919-715-0577

NORTH DAKOTA

State Offices:
Heidi Heitkamp
Office of Attorney General
600 E. Boulevard
Bismarck, ND 58505
Phone: 701-224-2210
Toll free in ND: 800-472-2600

Darrell Grossman, Director
Consumer Protection Division
Office of Attorney General
600 E. Boulevard
Bismarck, ND 58505
Phone: 701-224-3404
Toll free in ND: 800-472-2600

OHIO

State Offices:
Helen MacMurray
Consumer Frauds and Crimes Section
Office of Attorney General
30 E. Broad St.
State Office Tower, 25th Fl.
Columbus, OH 43266-0410
Phone: 614-466-4986 (complaints)
Toll free in OH: 800-282-0515
TDD: 614-466-1393

Robert F. Tongren
Office of Consumers' Counsel
77 S. High St., 15th Fl.
Columbus, OH 43266-0550
Toll free in OH: 800-282-9448
Voice/TDD: 614-466-9605

OKLAHOMA

State Offices:
Jane Wheeler
Assistant Attorney General
Office of Attorney General
Consumer Protection Unit
4545 N. Lincoln Blvd., Ste. 260
Oklahoma City, OK 73105
Phone: 405-521-4274
Phone: 405-521-2029 (consumer hotline)
Fax: 405-528-1867

Charles Jones, Administrator
Department of Consumer Credit
4545 N. Lincoln Blvd., Ste. 104
Oklahoma City, OK 73105-3408
Phone: 405-521-3653
Fax: 405-521-6740

OREGON

State Office:
Peter Sheperd, Attorney in Charge
Financial Fraud Section
Department of Justice
1162 Court St., NE
Salem, OR 97310
Phone: 503-378-4732
Fax: 503-373-7067

PENNSYLVANIA

State Offices:
Joseph Goldberg, Director
Bureau of Consumer Protection
Office of Attorney General
Strawberry Sq., 14th Fl.
Harrisburg, PA 17120
Phone: 717-787-9707
Toll free in PA: 800-441-2555

Irwin A. Popowsky, Consumer Advocate
Office of Consumer Advocate-Utilities
Office of Attorney General
1425 Strawberry Sq.
Harrisburg, PA 17120
Phone: 717-783-5048 (utilities only)
Fax: 717-783-7152

Michael Butler
Deputy Attorney General
Bureau of Consumer Protection
Office of Attorney General
1251 S. Cedar Crest Blvd., Ste. 309
Allentown, PA 18103
Phone: 610-821-6690

Mitchell Miller, Director
Bureau of Consumer Services
Pennsylvania Public Utility Commission
P.O. Box 3265
Harrisburg, PA 17105-3265
Phone: 717-783-1740
Toll free in PA: 800-782-1110
Fax: 717-787-4193

Jesse Harvey
Deputy Attorney General
Bureau of Consumer Protection
Office of Attorney General
919 State St., Rm. 203
Erie, PA 16501
Phone: 814-871-4371
Fax: 814-871-4848

E. Barry Creany
Senior Deputy Attorney General
Bureau of Consumer Protection
Office of the Attorney General
171 Lovell Ave., Suite 202
Ebensburg, PA 15931
Phone: 814-949-7900
Toll free in PA: 800-441-2555
Fax: 814-949-7942

John E. Kelly,
Deputy Attorney General
Bureau of Consumer Protection
Office of Attorney General
21 S. 12th St., 2nd Fl.
Philadelphia, PA 19107
Phone: 215-560-2414
Toll free in PA: 800-441-2555

Stephanie L. Royal
Deputy Attorney General
Bureau of Consumer Protection
Office of Attorney General
Manor Complex, 6th Fl.
564 Forbes Ave.
Pittsburgh, PA 15219
Phone: 412-565-5394
Toll free in PA: 800-441-2555

J.P. McGowan
Deputy Attorney General
Bureau of Consumer Protection
Office of Attorney General
214 Samters Bldg.
101 Penn Ave.
Scranton, PA 18503-2025
Phone: 717-963-4913
Fax: 717-963-3418

PUERTO RICO

Jose Antonio Alicia Rivera, Secretary
Department of Consumer Affairs
Minillas Station, P.O. Box 41059
Santurce, PR 00940-1059
Phone: 787-721-0940
Phone: 787-726-6570

Pedro R. Pierluisi, Secretary
Department of Justice
P.O. Box 192
San Juan, PR 00902
Phone: 787-721-2900

RHODE ISLAND

State Offices:
Steve Bucci, President
Consumer Credit Counseling Services
535 Centerville Rd., Ste. 103
Warwick, RI 02886
Phone: 401-732-1800
Toll free: 800-781-2227
Fax: 401-732-0250

Christine S. Jabour, Esq.
Consumer Protection Division
Department of Attorney General
72 Pine St.
Providence, RI 02903
Phone: 401-274-4400
Toll free in RI: 800-852-7776
Fax: 401-277-1331
TDD: 401-453-0410

SOUTH CAROLINA

State Offices:
Haviard Jones
Senior Assistant Attorney General
Office of Attorney General
P.O. Box 11549
Columbia, SC 29211
Phone: 803-734-3970
Fax: 803-734-3677

Philip S. Porter
Administrator, Consumer Advocate
Department of Consumer Affairs
P.O. Box 5757
Columbia, SC 29250-5757
Phone: 803-734-9452
Toll free in SC: 800-922-1594
TDD: 803-734-9455

W. Jefferson Bryson, Jr.
State Ombudsman
Office of Executive Policy and Program
1205 Pendleton St., Rm. 308
Columbia, SC 29201
Phone: 803-734-0457
Fax: 803-734-0546
TDD: 803-734-1147

SOUTH DAKOTA

State Office:
Division of Consumer Protection
Office of Attorney General
500 E. Capitol
State Capitol Bldg.
Pierre, SD 57501-5070
Phone: 605-773-4400
Toll free in SD: 800-300-1986
Fax: 605-773-4106
TDD: 605-773-6585

TENNESSEE

State Offices:
Mark Williams, Director
Division of Consumer Affairs
500 James Robertson Pkwy.
Nashville, TN 37243-0600
Phone: 615-741-4737
Toll free in TN: 800-342-8385
(All complaints must be sent to
the above address at Consumer
Affairs for processing)

Cynthia Carter
Deputy Attorney General
Division of Consumer Protection
Office of Attorney General
500 Charlotte Ave.
Nashville, TN 37243-0491
Phone: 615-741-3491
Fax: 615-532-2910

TEXAS

State Offices:
Tom Perkins
Assistant Attorney General and Chief
Consumer Protection Division
Office of Attorney General
P.O. Box 12548
Austin, TX 78711
Phone: 512-463-2070

Robert E. Reyna
Assistant Attorney General
Consumer Protection Division
Office of Attorney General
714 Jackson St., Ste. 800
Dallas, TX 75202-4506
Phone: 214-742-8944
Fax: 214-939-3930

Valli Jo Acosta
Assistant Attorney General
Consumer Protection Division
Office of Attorney General
6090 Surety Dr., Rm. 113
El Paso, TX 79905
Phone: 915-772-9476
Fax: 915-772-9046

Richard Tomlinson
Assistant Attorney General
Consumer Protection Division
Office of Attorney General
1019 Congress St., Ste. 1550
Houston, TX 77002-1702
Phone: 713-223-5886

Assistant Attorney General
Consumer Protection Division
Office of Attorney General
916 Main St., Ste. 806
Lubbock, TX 79401-3997
Phone: 806-747-5238
Fax: 806-747 6307

Ric Madrigal
Assistant Attorney General
Consumer Protection Division
Office of Attorney General
3201 N. McColl Rd., Ste. B
McAllen, TX 78501
Phone: 210-682-4547
Fax: 210-682-1957

Aaron Valenzuela
Assistant Attorney General
Consumer Protection Division
Office of Attorney General
115 E. Travis St., Ste. 925
San Antonio, TX 78205-1615
Phone: 210-224-1007

Office of Public Insurance Counsel
333 Guadalupe, Ste. 3-120
Austin, TX 78701
Phone: 512-322-4143
Fax: 512-322-4148

UTAH

State Office:
Francine A. Giani, Director
Division of Consumer Protection
Department of Commerce
160 E. 300 South
Box 146704
Salt Lake City, UT 84114-6704
Phone: 801-530-6601
Toll free in UT: 800-721-7233
Fax: 801-530-6001

VERMONT

State Offices:
John Hasen
Assistant Attorney General and Chief
Public Protection Division
Office of Attorney General
109 State St.
Montpelier, VT 05609-1001
Phone: 802-828-3171
Fax: 802-828-2154

Bruce Martell, Supervisor
Consumer Assurance Section
Department of Agriculture, Food and
Market
120 State St.
Montpelier, VT 05620-2901
Phone: 802-828-2436

VIRGIN ISLANDS

Vera Falu, Commissioner
Department of Licensing and
Consumer Affairs
Property and Procurement Bldg.
Subbase #1, Rm. 205
St. Thomas, VI 00802
Phone: 809-774-3130
Fax: 809-776-0605

VIRGINIA

State Offices:
Frank Seales, Jr., Chief
Antitrust & Consumer Litigation Section
Office of Attorney General
900 E. Main St.
Richmond, VA 23219
Phone: 804-786-2116
Fax: 804-371-2086/2087

Robert E. Colvin
Project Manager,
Office of Consumer Affairs
Department of Agriculture and
Consumer Services
Washington Bldg., Ste. 100
P.O. Box 1163
Richmond, VA 23219
Phone: 804-786-2042
Toll free in VA: 800-552-9963
Fax: 804-371-7479
TDD: 804-371-6344

WASHINGTON

State Offices:
Mala Nagarajan, Supervisor
Consumer Protection Division
Office of the Attorney General
103 E. Holly St., Ste. 308
Bellingham, WA 98225
Phone: 360-738-6185
Toll free in WA: 800-551-4636
TDD Toll free: 800-276-9883
TDD: 206-464-7293

Christy Martinez, Supervisor
Consumer Protection Division
Office of the Attorney General
500 N. Morain St., Ste. 1250
Kennewick, WA 99336-2607
Phone: 509-734-7140
Toll free in WA: 800-551-4636
TDD Toll free in WA: 800-276-9883
TDD: 206-464-7293

Larry D. Keyes, Supervisor
Consumer Protection Division
Office of the Attorney General
P.O. Box 40118
Olympia, WA 98504-0118
Phone: 360-753-6210
Toll free in WA: 800-551-4636
TDD Toll free in WA: 800-276-9883
TDD: 206-464-7293

Sally Sterling
Director Consumer and Business
Fair Practices Division
Office of the Attorney General
900 4th Ave., Ste. 2000
Seattle, WA 98164
Phone: 206-464-6684
Toll free in WA: 800-551-4636
TDD Toll free: 800-276-9883
TDD: 206-464-7293

Owen Clarke, Chief
Consumer and Business
Fair Practices Division
Office of the Attorney General
West 1116 Riverside Ave.
Spokane, WA 99201
Phone: 509-456-3123
Toll free in WA: 800-551-4636
Fax: 509-458-3548
TDD Toll free: 800-276-9883
TDD: 206-464-7293

Cynthia Lanphear,
Consumer and Business
Office of the Attorney General
1019 Pacific Ave., 3rd Fl.
Tacoma, WA 98402-4411
Phone: 206-593-2904
Toll free in WA: 800-551-4636
Fax: 206-593-2449
TDD Toll free: 800-276-9883
TDD: 206-464-7293

June Bachman, Supervisor
Consumer Protection Division
Office of the Attorney General
500 W. 8th St., Ste. 55
Vancouver, WA 98660
 Phone: 360-690-4751
Toll free in WA: 800-551-4636
Fax: 360-690-4762
TDD: 206-464-7293
TDD Toll free in WA: 800-276-9883

WEST VIRGINIA

State Offices:
Jill Miles
Deputy Attorney General
Consumer Protection Division
Office of Attorney General
812 Quarrier St., 6th Fl.
Charleston, WV 25301
Phone: 304-558-8986
Toll free in WV: 800-368-8808
Fax: 304-558-0184

Karl H. Angell, Jr. Director
Division of Labor
Weights and Measures Section
570 MacCorkle Ave.
St. Albans, WV 25177
Phone: 304-348-7890
Fax: 304-722-0605

WISCONSIN

State Offices:
William Oemichen, Administrator
Division of Trade and
Consumer Protection
Department of Agriculture, Trade
and Consumer Protection
2811 Agriculture Dr.
P.O. Box 8911
Madison, WI 53708
Phone: 608-224-4950
Toll free in WI: 800-422-7128
Fax: 608-224-4939

Margaret Quaid, Regional Supervisor
Division of Trade and Consumer Protection
Department of Agriculture, Trade
and Consumer Protection
927 Loring St.
Altoona, WI 54720
Phone: 715-839-3848
Toll free in WI: 800-422-7128
Fax: 715-839-1645

Judy Cardin
Regional Supervisor
Division of Trade
and Consumer Protection
Department of Agriculture, Trade
and Consumer Protection
200 N. Jefferson St., Ste. 146A
Green Bay, WI 54301
Phone: 414-448-5111
Toll free in WI: 800-422-7128
TDD: 608-224 5058

Elmer Prenzlow
Regional Supervisor
Consumer Protection Regional Office
Department of Agriculture, Trade
and Consumer Protection
10930 W. Potter Rd., Ste. C
Milwaukee, WI 53226-3450
Phone: 414-266-1231

WYOMING

State Office:
Mark Moran,
Assistant Attorney General
Office of Attorney General
123 State Capitol Bldg.
Cheyenne, WY 82002
Phone: 307-777-7874
Fax: 307-777-6869

BETTER BUSINESS BUREAUS

Better Business Bureaus (BBBs) are private dispute resolution centers funded by local businesses. They attempt to resolve problems between consumers and businesses informally. BBBs accept written complaints and try to get the two sides to reach agreement, through either mediation or arbitration.

BBBs handle problems with contractors, large and small; retailers, auto repair shops; and others. They also maintain records of the number of complaints filed against local companies. If you have doubts about any local business, call to ask how many complaints have been filed against it. Also ask about the proper form to use before sending in a complaint.

If you need help with a consumer question or complaint, call your local BBB to ask about its services. Or you can go on-line to acquire information about the BBB through the Internet, located at http://www.bbb.org. The BBB World Wide Web server features consumer fraud and scam alerts and provides information about BBB programs, services and locations.

The Council of Better Business Bureaus, the umbrella organization for the BBBs, also provides programs and publications for consumers. The Council can assist with complaints about the truthfulness and accuracy of national advertising claims, including children's advertising; provide reports on national soliciting charities; and help to settle disputes with automobile manufacturers through the BBB AUTO LINE program (see page 123).

The list of Better Business Bureaus is excerpted from the *1997 Consumer Resource Handbook,* published by the U.S. Office of Consumer Affairs.

National Office

COUNCIL OF BETTER BUSINESS
BUREAUS, INC.
4200 Wilson Blvd.
Arlington, VA 22203
Phone: 703-276-0100

Local Bureaus

ALABAMA

1210 S. 20th St.
P.O. Box 55268
Birmingham, AL 35205
Phone: 205-558-2222

1528 Peachtree Ln., Ste. 1
Cullman, AL 35057
Phone: 205-737-0539

118 Woodburn
Dothan, AL 36301
Phone: 334-794-0492

102 Court St., Ste. 512
Florence, AL 35620
Toll free: 800-239-1642

107 Lincoln St., NE
P.O. Box 383
Huntsville, AL 3 5804
Phone: 205-533-1640

100 N. Royal St.
Mobile, AL 36602-3295
Phone: 334-433-5494

60 Commerce St., Ste. 806
Montgomery, AL 36104-3559
Phone: 334-262-5606

ALASKA

2805 Bering St., Ste. 5
Anchorage, AK 99503-3819
Phone: 907-562-0704

P.O. Box 74675
Fairbanks, AK 99707
Phone: 907-451-0222

ARIZONA

4428 N. 12th St.
Phoenix, AZ 85014-4585
Phone: 900-225-5222 ($.95/min.)
Phone: 602-240-3473 (flat fee of $3.80)

3620 N. 1st Ave., Ste. 136
Tucson, AZ 85719
Phone: 520-888-5353

ARKANSAS

1415 S. University
Little Rock, AR 72204-2605
Phone: 501-664-7274

CALIFORNIA

705 18th St.
Bakersfield, CA 93301
Phone: 805-322-2074

290 N. 10th St., Ste. 206
Colton, CA 92324-3052
Phone: 900-225-5222 ($.95/min.)

6101 Ball Rd., Ste. 309
Cypress, CA 90630-3966
Phone: 900-225-5222 ($.95/min.)

2519 W. Shaw, Ste. 106
Fresno, CA 93711
Phone: 209-222-8111

3727 W. 6th St., Ste. 607
Los Angeles, CA 90020
Phone: 900-225-5222 ($.95/min.)

510 16th St., Ste. 550
Oakland, CA 94612-1584
Phone: 510-238-1000

400 S St.
Sacramento, CA 95814-6997
Phone: 916-443-6843

5050 Murphy Canyon, Ste. 110
San Diego, CA 92123
Phone: 619-496-2131

1530 Meridian, Ste. 110
San Jose, CA 95125
Phone: 408-445-3000

400 S. El Camino Real, Ste. 350
San Mateo, CA 94402-1706
Phone: 415-696-1240

213 Santa Barbara St.
Santa Barbara, CA 93102
Phone: 805-963-8657

11 S. San Joaquin St.
Stockton, CA 9 5202-3202
Phone: 209-948-4880

COLORADO

3622 N. El Paso
P.O. Box 7970
Colorado Springs, CO 80933-7970
Phone: 719-636-1155

1780 S. Bellaire, Ste. 700
Denver, CO 80222-4350
Phone: 303-758-2100

1730 S. College Ave., Ste. 303
Fort Collins, CO 80525-1073
907-484-1348
Phone: 370-778-2809 (Cheyenne)

119 W. 6th St., Ste. 203
Pueblo, CO 81003-3119
Phone: 719-542-6464

CONNECTICUT

Parkside Bldg.
821 N. Main St.
Wallingford, CT 06492-2420
Phone: 203-269-2700

DELAWARE

2055 Limestone Rd., Ste. 200
Wilmington, DE 19808-5532
Phone: 302-996-9200

DISTRICT OF COLUMBIA

1012 14th St., NW, 9th Fl.
Washington, DC 20005-3410
Phone: 202-393-8000

FLORIDA

5830 142nd Ave., North Ste. B (34620)
P.O. Box 7950
Clearwater, FL 34618-7950
Phone: 813-842-5459 (Pasco City)
Phone: 813-535-5522 (Pinellas County)
Phone: 813-854-1154 (Hills, Tampa)
Phone: 813-957-0093 (Sarasota, Manatee)
Toll free: 800-525-1447 (Hernando)

2710 Swamp Cabbage Court
Fort Myers, FL 33901-9333
Phone: 900-225-5222 ($.95/min.)

16291 N.W. 57th Ave.
Miami, FL 33014-6709
Phone: 900-225-5222 ($.95/min.)

4900 Bayou Blvd., Ste. 112
Pensacola, FL 32597-1511
Phone: 904-494-0222

1950 Port St. Lucie Blvd., Ste. 211
Port St. Lucie, FL 34952-5579
Phone: 407-337-2083

580 Village Blvd., Ste. 340
West Palm Beach, FL 33409
Phone: 561-686-2200

1011 N. Wymore Rd., Ste. 204
Winter Park, FL 32789-1736
Phone: 407-621-3300

GEORGIA

204 N. Jackson
Albany, GA 31706-3241
Phone: 912-883-0744

100 Edgewood Ave., Ste. 1012
Atlanta, GA 30303-3075
Phone: 404-688-4910

301 7th St.
P.O. Box 2085
Augusta, GA 30903-2085
Phone: 706-722-1574

208 13th St.
P.O. Box 2587 (31902-2587)
Columbus, GA 31901-2137
Phone: 706-324-0712

301 Mulberry St., Ste. 102
Macon, GA 31201
Phone: 912-742-7999

6606 Abercorn St., Ste. 108-C
Savannah, GA 31405-5817
Phone: 912-354-7521

HAWAII

1600 Kapiolani Blvd., Ste. 201
Honolulu, HI 96814-3801
Phone: 808-941-5222

IDAHO

1333 W. Jefferson
Boise, ID 83702-5320
Phone: 208-342-4649

1575 South Blvd.
Idaho Falls, ID 83404-5926
Phone: 208-523-9754

ILLINOIS

330 N. Wabash
Chicago, IL 60611
Phone: 900-225-5222 ($.95/min.)

3024 W. Lake
Peoria, IL 61615-3770
Phone: 309-688-3741

810 E. State St., 3rd Fl.
Rockford, IL 61104-1001
Phone: 900-225-5222 ($.95/min.)

INDIANA

722 W. Bristol St., Ste. H-2
P.O. Box 405
Elkhart, IN 46515-0405
Phone: 219-262-8996

4004 Morgan Ave., Ste. 201
Evansville, IN 47715-2265
Phone: 812-473-0202

1203 Webster St.
Fort Wayne, IN 46802-3493
Phone: 219-423-4433

4189 Cleveland St.
Gary, IN 46408
Phone: 219-980-1511
Phone: 219-769-8053

22 E. Washington St., Ste. 200
Indianapolis, IN 46204-3584
Phone: 317-488-2222

207 Dixie Way North, Ste. 130
South Bend, IN 46637-3360
Phone: 219-277-9121

IOWA

852 Middle Rd., Ste. 290
Bettendorf, IA 52722-4100
Phone: 319-355-6344

505 5th Ave., Ste. 615
Des Moines, IA 50309-2375
Phone: 515-243-8137

505 6th St., Ste. 417
Sioux City, IA 51101
Phone: 712-252-4501

KANSAS

501 S.E. Jefferson, Ste. 24
Topeka, KS 66607-1190
Phone: 913-232-0454

328 Laura
P.O. Box 11707-1190
Wichita, KS 67211
Phone: 316-263-3146

KENTUCKY

410 W. Vine St., Ste. 280
Lexington, KY 40507-1616
Phone: 606-259-1008

844 S. 4th St.
Louisville, KY 40203-2186
Phone: 502-583-6546

LOUISIANA

1605 Murray St., Ste. 117
Alexandria, LA 71301-6875
Phone: 318-473-4494

2055 Wooddale Blvd.
Baton Rouge, LA 70806-1546
Phone: 504-926-3010

3038 Park, NE, Ste. 204
Houma, LA 70360-6354
Phone: 504-868-3456

100 Huggins Rd.
P.O. Box 30297
Lafayette, LA 70593-0297
Phone: 318-981-3497

3941-L Ryan St.
P.O. Box 7314
Lake Charles, LA 70606-7314
Phone: 318-478-6253

141 Desiard St., Ste. 808
Monroe, LA 71201-7380
Phone: 318-387-4600

1539 Jackson Ave., Ste. 400
New Orleans, LA 70130-5843
Phone: 504-581-6222

3612 Youree Dr.
Shreveport, LA 71105-2122
Phone: 318-861-6417

MAINE

812 Stevens Ave.
Portland, ME 04103-2648
Phone: 207-878-2715

MARYLAND

2100 Huntingdon Ave.
Baltimore, MD 21211-3215
Phone: 900-225-5222 ($.95/min.)

MASSACHUSETTS

20 Park Plaza, Ste. 820
Boston, MA 02116-4344
Phone: 617-426-9000

293 Bridge St., Ste. 320
Springfield, MA 01103-1402
Phone: 413-734-3114

32 Franklin St.
P.O. Box 16555
Worcester, MA 01608-1900
Phone: 508-755-2548

MICHIGAN

40 Pearl, NW, Ste. 354
Grand Rapids, MI 49503
Phone: 616-774-8236

30555 Southfield Rd., Ste. 200
Southfield, MI 48076-7751
Phone: 810-644-9100

MINNESOTA

2706 Gannon Rd.
St. Paul, MN 55116-2600
Phone: 612-699-1111

MISSISSIPPI

4500 155 North, Ste. 287
P.O. Box 12745
Jackson, MS 39236-2745
Phone: 601-987-8282

MISSOURI

306 E. 12th St., Ste. 1024
Kansas City, MO 64106-2418
Phone: 816-421-7800

12 Sunnen Dr., Ste. 121
St. Louis, MO 63143
Phone: 314-645-3300

205 Park Central East, Ste. 509
Springfield, MO 65806-1326
Phone: 417-862-4222

NEBRASKA

3633 O St., Ste. 1
Lincoln, NE 68510-1670
Phone: 402-476-8855

2237 N. 91st Ct.
Omaha, NE 68134-6022
Phone: 402-391-7612

NEVADA

1022 E. Sahara Ave.
Las Vegas, NV 89104-1515
Phone: 702-735-6900

991 Bible Way
P.O. Box 21269
Reno, NV 89515-1269
Phone: 702-322-0657

NEW HAMPSHIRE

410 S. Main St., Ste. 3
Concord, NH 03301-3483
Phone: 603-224-1991

NEW JERSEY

400 Lanidex Plaza
Parsippany, NJ 07054-2797
Phone: 201-581-1313

1721 Route 37
East Toms River, NJ 08753-8239
Phone: 908-270-5577

1700 Whitehorse-Hamilton Sq.,Ste. D-5
Trenton, NJ 08690-3596
Phone: 609-588-0808

16 Maple Ave.
P.O. Box 303
Westmont, NJ 08108-0303
Phone: 609-854-8467

NEW MEXICO

2625 Pennsylvania, NE, Ste. 2050
Albuquerque, NM 87110-3657
Phone: 505-884-0500

308 N. Locke
Farmington, NM 87401-5855
Phone: 505-326-6501

201 N. Church, Ste. 330
Las Cruces, NM 88001-3548
Phone: 505-524-3130

NEW YORK

346 Delaware Ave.
Buffalo, NY 14202-1899
Phone: 900-225-5222 ($.95/min.)

266 Main St.
Farmingdale, NY 11735-2618
Phone: 900-225-5222 ($.95/min.)

257 Park Ave., South
New York, NY 10010-7384
Phone: 900-225-5222 ($.95/min.)

847 James St., Ste. 200
Syracuse, NY 13202-2552
Phone: 900-225-522 ($.95/min.)

30 Glenn St.
White Plains, NY 10603-3213
Phone: 900-225-5222 ($.95/min.)

NORTH CAROLINA

1200 BB&T Bldg.
Asheville, NC 28801-3418
Phone: 704-253-2392

5200 Park Rd., Ste. 202
Charlotte, NC 28209-3650
Phone: 704-527-0012

3608 W. Friendly Ave.
Greensboro, NC 27410-4895
Phone: 910-852-4240

3125 Poplarwood Ct., Ste. 308
Raleigh, NC 27604-1080
Phone: 919-872-9240

Eden Place 8366 Drena Dr.
P.O. Box 69
Sherrils Ford, NC 28673-0069
Phone: 704-478-5622

500 W. 5th St., Ste. 202
Winston-Salem, NC 27101-2728
Phone: 910-725-8384

OHIO

222 W. Market St.
Akron, OH 44303-2111
Phone: 330-253-4590

1434 Cleveland Ave., NW (44703)
P.O. Box 8017
Canton, OH 44711-8017
Phone: 330-454-9401

898 Walnut St.
Cincinnati, OH 45202-2097
Phone: 513-421-3015

2217 E. 9th St., Ste. 200
Cleveland, OH 44115-1299
Phone: 216-241-7678

1335 Dublin St., Ste. 30-A
Columbus, OH 43215-1000
Phone: 614-486-6336

40 W. 4th St., Ste. 1250
Dayton, OH 45402-1828
Phone: 513-222-5825

112 N.W. High St.
P.O. Box 269
Lima, OH 45802-0269
Phone: 419-223-7010

425 Jefferson Ave., Ste. 909
Toledo, OH 43604-1055
Phone: 419-241-6276

600 Mahoning Bank Bldg.
P.O. Box 1495
Youngstown, OH 44501-1495
Phone: 330-744-3111

OKLAHOMA

17 S. Dewey
Oklahoma City, OK 73102-2400
Phone: 405-239-6081

6711 S. Yale, Ste. 230
Tulsa, OK 74136-3327
Phone: 918-492-1266

OREGON

333 S.W. 5th Ave., Ste. 300
Portland, OR 97204
Phone: 503-226-3981

PENNSYLVANIA

528 N. New St.
Bethlehem, PA 18018-5789
Phone: 610-866-8780

29 E. King St., Ste. 322
Lancaster, PA 17602-2852
Phone: 900-225-5222 ($.95/min.)

1930 Chestnut St.
P.O. Box 2297
Philadelphia, PA 19103-0297
Phone: 900-225-5222 ($.95/min.)

300 6th Ave., Ste. 100-UL
Pittsburgh, PA 15222-2511
Phone: 412-456-2700

129 N. Washington Ave.
P.O. Box 993
Scranton, PA 18501-0993
Phone: 717-342-9129

PUERTO RICO

1608 Bori St.
San Juan, PR 00927-6100
Phone: 809-756-5400

RHODE ISLAND

120 Lavan St.
Warwick, RI 02887-1071
Phone: 401-785-1212

SOUTH CAROLINA

2330 Devine St.
P.O. Box 8326
Columbia, SC 29202-8326
Phone: 803-254-2525

307-B Falls St.
Greenville, SC 29601-2829
Phone: 803-242-5052

1601 N. Oak St., Ste. 101
Myrtle Beach, SC 29577-1601
Phone: 803-626-6881

TENNESSEE

P.O. Box 1178 TCA
Blountville, TN 37617-1178
Phone: 423-325-6616

1010 Market St., Ste. 200
Chattanooga, TN 37402-2614
Phone: 423-266-6144

2633 Kingston Pike, Ste. 2
P.O. Box 10327
Knoxville, TN 37939-0327
Phone: 423-522-2552

6525 Quall Hollow, Ste. 410
P.O. Box 17036
Memphis, TN 38178-0036
Phone: 901-759-1300

414 Union St., Ste. 1830
Nashville, TN 37219-1778
Phone: 615-242-4BBB

TEXAS

3300 S. 14th St., Ste. 307
Abilene, TX 79605-5052
Phone: 915-691-1533

1000 S. Polk
P.O. Box 1905
Amarillo, TX 79105-1905
Phone: 806-379-6222

2101 So. IH35, Ste. 302
Austin, TX 78741-3854
Phone: 512-445-2911

476 Oakland Ave.
P.O. Box 2988
Beaumont, TX 77704-2988
Phone: 409-835-5348

4346 Carter Creek Pky.
Bryan, TX 77802-4413
Phone: 409-260-2222

216 Park Ave.
Corpus Christi, TX 78401
Phone: 512-887-4949

2001 Bryan St., Ste. 850
Dallas, TX 75201-3093
Phone: 900-225-5222 ($95/min.)

State National Plaza, Ste. 1101
El Paso, TX 79901
Phone: 915-577-0191

1612 Summit Ave., Ste. 260
Fort Worth, TX 76102-5978
Phone: 817-332-7585

5225 Katz Freeway, Ste. 500
Houston, TX 77007
Phone: 900-225-5222 ($.95/min.)

916 Main St., Ste. 800
Lubbock, TX 79401-3910
Phone: 806-763-0459

10100 County Rd., 118 West
P.O. Box 60206
Midland, TX 79711-0206
Phone: 915-563-1880

3121 Executive Dr.
P.O. Box 3366
San Angelo, TX 76902-3366
Phone: 915-949-2986

1800 N.E. Loop 410, Ste. 400
San Antonio, TX 78217-5296
Phone: 210-828-9441

3600 Old Bullard Rd., Ste. 103-A
P.O. Box 6652
Tyler, TX 75711-6652
Phone: 903-581-5704

6801 Sanger Ave., Ste. 125
P.O. Box 7203
Waco, TX 76714-7203
Phone: 817-772-7530

609 International Blvd.
P.O. Box 69
Weslaco, TX 78599-0069
Phone: 210-968-3678

4245 Kemp Blvd., Ste. 900
Wichita Falls, TX 76308-2830
Phone: 817-691-1172

UTAH

1588 S. Main St.
Salt Lake City, UT 84115-5382
Phone: 801-487-4656

VERMONT

(Contact Boston office)
Toll free: 800-4BBB-811 (802-Vermont only)

VIRGINIA

11903 Main St.
Fredericksburg, VA 22408
Phone: 540-373-9872

3608 Tidewater Dr.
Norfolk, VA 23509-1499
Phone: 804-627-5651

701 E. Franklin, Ste. 712
Richmond, VA 23219-2332
Phone: 804-648-0016

31 W. Campbell Ave.
Roanoke, VA 24011-1301
Phone: 540-342-3455

WASHINGTON

1401 N. Union, Ste. 105
Kennewick, WA 99336-3819
Phone: 509-783-0892

4800 S. 188th St., Ste. 222
P.O. Box 68926
Sea Tac, WA 98168-0926
Phone: 900-225-5222 ($4 call)

East 123 Indiana, Ste. 106
Spokane, WA 99207-2356
Phone: 509-328-2100

32 N. 3rd St., Ste. 410
P.O. Box 1584
Yakima, WA 98901
Phone: 509-248-1326

WISCONSIN

740 N. Plankinton Ave.
Milwaukee, WI 53203-2478
Phone: 414-273-1600

MEDIA HELP

Some newspapers, TV and radio stations help consumers having problems with local merchants or utilities with a "hot line" or "action" service. If trying to resolve the problem with a business on your own fails, find out if your area has a media-sponsored consumer action program. Media programs of this sort are often successful because businesses involved act quickly to avoid bad publicity. You can find out if your community has such a media-sponsored program by simply calling local newspapers, TV and radio stations, and asking if they have a consumer reporter.

Call For Action, an international consumer help organization, may also be able to assist you in resolving problems with local merchants or utility companies. This service is free and their offices in the United States are affiliated with a television or radio station. So if you have a consumer problem, call or write to the office nearest to you. The following list contains the location, phone number and hours of operation of the Call For Action offices in the U.S.

NATIONAL OFFICE

CALL FOR ACTION
Network Hotline
5272 River Rd., Ste. 300
Bethesda, MD 20813
Phone: 301-657-7490
M-F 10 a.m. - 3 p.m. ET

LOCAL OFFICES
(Alphabetically by city)

WTAJ-TV
Call For Action
5000 6th Ave.
Altoona, PA 16602
Phone: 814-944-9336
M-F 1 p.m. - 3 p.m. ET

WBAP Radio
Call For Action
2221 E. Lamar Blvd.
Arlington, TX 76006
Phone: 817-695-2820
M-F 10 a.m. - 12 p.m. CT

KLBJ Radio
Call For Action
8309 North I-35
Austin, TX 78753
Phone: 512-833-9232
T-Th 11 a.m. - 1 p.m. CT

WTOP Radio
Call For Action
5272 River Rd., Ste. 300
Bethesda, MD 20813
Phone: 301-652-4357
T-F 11 a.m. -1 p.m. ET

WBZ-TV & Radio
Call For Action
1170 Soldiers Field Rd.
Boston, MA 02134
Phone: 617-787-7070
M-F 11 a.m. - 1:30 p.m. ET

WIVB-TV
Call For Action
2077 Elmwood Ave.
Buffalo, NY 14207
Phone: 716-879-4900
M-F 11 a.m. - 1 p.m. ET

WBBM-TV
Call For Action
630 N. McClurg Ct.
Chicago, IL 60611
Phone: 312-951-1572
M-F 11 a.m. - 1 p.m. CT

WJW-TV
Call For Action
5800 S. Marginal Rd.
Cleveland, OH 44103
Phone: 216-391-4508
M, W, Th 10 a.m.-1 p.m.
M, Tu 5:30 p.m. - 6:30 p.m. ET

KWQC-TV
Call For Action
805 Brady St.
Davenport, IA 52803
Phone: 319-383-7006
M-F 9 a.m. - 11 a.m. CT

WRAL-TV
Call For Action
112 N. Queen St.
Box G
Durham, NC 27701
Phone: 919-688-9306
M-F 10:30 a.m. - 2:30 p.m. ET

WINK-TV
Call For Action
2824 Palm Beach Blvd.
Fort Myers, FL 33916
Phone: 813-334-4357
M-Th 11 a.m. - 1 p.m. ET

WOWK-TV
Call For Action
555 5th Ave.
Huntington, WV 25701
Phone: 304-697-9695
M, W 11 a.m. - 1 p.m. ET

KCTV5
Call For Action
P.O. Box 5555
Kansas City, MO 66205
Phone: 913-831-1919
Summer: T, W, Th 9:30 a.m. - 4:30 p.m. CT
Winter: M-Th 9:30 a.m. - 4 p.m. CT

WABC Radio
Call For Action
2 Penn Plaza, 17th Fl.
New York, NY 10121
Phone: 212-268-5626
M-F 11 a.m. - 1 p.m. ET

KWY-TV & Radio
Call For Action
Independence Mall East
Philadelphia, PA 19106
Phone: 215-238-4500
M-F 11 a.m. - 1 p.m. ET

KDKA Radio
Call For Action
1 Gateway Ctr.
Pittsburgh, PA 15222
Phone: 412-333-9370
M-F 10 a.m. - 1 p.m. ET

KTVI-TV
Call For Action
5915 Berthold Ave.
St. Louis, MO 63110
Phone: 214-282-2222
Toll free: 800-782-2222 (Illinois only)
M-F 11 a.m. - 1 p.m. CT

KCBS Radio
Call For Action
1 Embarcadero Ctr.
San Francisco, CA 94111
Phone: 415-478-3300
M-F 11 a.m. - 1 p.m. PT

WXYZ & WJR Radio
Call For Action
P.O. Box 789
20777 W. Ten Mile Rd.
Southfield, MI 48037
Phone: 810-827-1107
M-F 11 a.m. - 1 p.m. ET

WTVT-TV
Call For Action
3213 W. Kennedy Blvd.
Tampa, FL 33631
Phone: 813-870-7113
M-F 11 a.m. - 1 p.m. ET

WTVG-TV
Call For Action
4247 Dorr St.
Toledo, OH 43607
Phone: 419-534-3838
T, W, 10 a.m. - 12 p.m. ET
M 5:30 p.m. - 6:30 p.m. ET

CREDIT PROBLEMS & REPORTING

When the plastic jug replaced the milkman's glass bottle back in the 1950s, few of us could imagine the "plastic" revolution that was about to sweep over us. Who would have concluded then that plastic would not only take over the container industry (and scores of other industries as well), but would replace money itself?

Yet today, consumer credit—typified by the ubiquitous credit card—is at an all-time high. So much does credit dominate our economy that entire companies have been set up to track people's credit lives in order to help merchants and bankers determine to whom to grant or deny credit and how much. This system has made your credit history one of the most important records for you to monitor.

Credit bureaus build and maintain computerized records of how much you have borrowed, your line of credit and your payment history—whether you have any court judgments against you, for example. Your current creditors can access your credit report at any time, but potential lenders have access to it only if you give written permission. If the credit bureau issues a report that the potential lender does not like, the lender may turn you down.

Your good credit is a valuable asset that can mean the difference between having access to goods and services and being forced to pay cash for every purchase. Due to credit problems, or even a mistake on your credit report, you may not be able to buy a house or car, get a credit card or anything else that requires a credit check. Therefore, it is essential that you make sure your credit report is correct, and fix any credit problems you may have.

Listed below are a number of places you can go for more information about credit, your credit record, or to get help fixing it.

Credit Counseling

The Consumer Credit Counseling Service (CCCS)

If you get into credit card trouble, you can contact the Consumer Credit Counseling Service (CCCS), a nonprofit organization. CCCS will put you on a budget and negotiate with your creditors on your behalf to work out a repayment plan for your debts. Every state has local CCCS branches. For a referral to the CSSS office nearest you, contact:

The National Foundation for Consumer Credit
8611 2nd Ave., Ste. 100
Silver Spring, MD, 20910
Phone: 301-589-5600
Toll free: 800-388-2227

Credit Repair Organizations

Review your credit report at least once a year and several months before making a major purchase, such as buying a home or automobile. A copy of your credit report or credit history can be obtained from any of the three major credit bureaus listed below. To make sure that all include the same information, it's a good idea to order a report from each bureau. If you find errors on your report, contact a credit repair organization (CRO) or try to correct the mistake yourself.

If you contact a CRO, be careful. As with any industry, there are legitimate CROs and fraudulent ones. Before engaging one, ask your local Better Business Bureau about its business history (see Chapter 3).

If you decide to correct the problem on your own, look for a "dispute form" that should have come with each copy of your credit report. Simply complete this form and return it to the credit bureau. The bureau will contact the company you have a disagreement with and within 30 days either update your report or notify you that the information was verified as reported and will not be changed. You can complain to the Federal Trade Commission (see page 120 for address) if you feel your credit report has been mishandled or that your request for correction has been ignored.

The cost of a credit report averages $8 to $10.

Equifax
Box 105873
Atlanta, GA, 30348
Toll free: 800-685-1111
Note: If you were denied credit in the past 60 days, you are entitled to a free copy; otherwise the cost is $8 per report.

Trans Union
Consumer Relations Dept.
Box 390
Springfield, PA 19064
Toll free: 800-916-8800
Note: If you were denied credit in the past 60 days, you are entitled to a free copy; otherwise the cost is $8 per report.

Experian (formerly TRW)
National Consumer Relations Center
Box 2104
Kileen, TX 75310-2104
Toll free: 800-682-7654
Note: If you were denied credit in the past 60 days, you are entitled to a free copy; otherwise the cost is $8 per report for most states, $2 in ME, $5 in CT.

Organizations

Federal Trade Commission
The Federal Trade Commission (FTC) is the federal agency that writes and enforces the advertising and trade rules businesses are required to abide by. It also protects consumers from unfair or deceptive business practices. It accepts written complaints and sends out free publications, such as:

- Credit Billing Problems? Use FCBA (Fair Credit Billing Act)
- Fix Your Own Credit Problems and Save Money
- Fair Debt Collection.

Complaint letters should be directed to:

Federal Trade Commission
Correspondence Dept., Rm. 692
Washington, DC 20580
Note: For free publications call 202-326-2222.

Bankcard Holders of America
Many issues that involve credit cards are consumer-oriented concerns that are not legal matters. For example, how do you get lower interest rates? What is the best way to manage credit? Can you get a credit card that does not charge an annual fee? Direct these and similar questions to the nonprofit organization, Bankcard Holders of America, an activist and educational association for credit card consumers. For more information, write:

Bankcard Holders of America
524 Branch Dr.
Salem, VA 24153
Phone: 540-389-5445

ORGANIZATIONS

Bankcard Holders of America
524 Branch Dr.
Salem, VA 24153
Phone: 540-389-5445

This is a nonprofit education and advocacy group that works on behalf of credit card consumers. It provides free information and lobbies for legislation that protects the rights of credit-card users.

Center for Science in the Public Interest
1875 Connecticut Ave., NW, Ste. 300
Washington, DC 20009
Phone: 202-332-9110

CSPI, a nonprofit, tax-exempt group funded through the sale of reports including *Eater's Digest,* provides the public with clear and reliable information about food issues, particularly government regulations concerning food and food processing industries.

Consumer Energy Council of America
2000 L St., NW, Ste. 802
Washington, DC 20036
Phone: 202-659-0404

CECA is a diverse coalition of organizations concerned with U.S. energy policy. Its research and advocacy agendas are directed toward issues including the influence of energy prices on public policy, the development of alternative energy sources and the management of existing energy sources.

Consumer Federation of America
1424 16th St., NW, Ste. 604
Washington, DC 20036
Phone: 202-387-6121

CFA, a federation of over 200 national, state and local organizations, strives to provide a voice for consumers through the gathering of facts, analysis of issues and dissemination of information to legislators, regulators and the general public. It lobbies Congress on issues including product liability, banking and energy legislation.

Consumers Union
1666 Connecticut Ave., NW, Ste. 310
Washington, DC 20009
Phone: 202-462-6262

CU, the publisher of *Consumer Reports Magazine*, is an independent, nonprofit organization that provides the public with information, education and counseling on consumer goods and services and the expenditure of family income. The Union also initiates and helps with individual and group efforts to create and improve decent living standards. The Washington office represents consumers interest in federal legislative and judicial proceedings.

National Consumers League
1701 K St., NW, Ste. 1200
Washington, DC 20006
Phone: 202-835-3323

NCL, the oldest consumer organization in the country, monitors the effects of the actions of Congress and federal agencies on consumers, both in the marketplace and work place. Its focal areas include health care, food and drug safety, fraud and consumer education, telecommunications, work-place privacy and child labor.

CONSUMER HOTLINES

Some of the hotlines below are listed in other sections of this book.

Auto Safety Hotline
Toll free: 800-424-9393

Better Business Bureau - Auto Line
Toll free: 800-955-5100

Boys Town
Toll free: 800-448-3000 (crisis hotline for boys, girls & parents)

Consumer Affairs National HelpLine
Toll free: 800-664-4435 (clearinghouse for consumer complaint handling, M-F, 10 a.m - 2 p.m.)

Consumer Credit Counseling Services
Toll free: 800-388-CCCS

Consumer Product Safety Commission
Toll free: 800-638-2772

Council of Better Business Bureaus, Inc.
Phone: 703-276-0100

Investment Fraud Hotline
Toll free: 800-676-4632

National Flood Insurance Hotline
Toll free: 800-638-6620

Postal Crime Hotline
Toll free: 800-654-8896

U. S. Department of Consumer Affairs
Toll free: 800-424-5197

WEB SITES

Better Business Bureau
URL: http://www.bbb.org/bbb/index.html
Home page for the Better Business Bureau. Site features consumer information and advisories, plus you can file a complaint against a business online.

Consumer Information Catalog
URL: http://www.pueblo.gsa.gov/
See profile on page 68

Consumer Law Page
URL: http://consumerlawpage.com/
Law firm sponsored web site features articles of interest to consumers, hundreds of free consumer information brochures and over 1000 links to other useful sites.

Consumer Product Safety Commission
URL: http://www.cpsc.gov/
See profile on page 68

Consumer World
URL: http://www.consumerworld.org/
Site offers a wealth of consumer information, including consumer advisories, product price comparisons, and links to other helpful sites.

Families USA Foundation
URL: http://www.familiesusa.org/
Web site features reports and other materials on health care reform and long-term care issues.

Insure Market
URL: http://www.insuremarket.com/
Comprehensive information about life, auto, and home insurance and valuable planning strategies to prepare for one's life. Connect with agents, compare quotes and purchase policies from the nation's leading insurance companies.

National Consumers League
URL: http://www.fraud.org/ifw.htm
NCL web site gives Internet users information against cybercrooks and alerts them to the 10 most common scams, including work-at-home schemes, prizes and sweepstakes, credit card offers and more.

National Fraud Information Center
URL: http://www.fraud.org/
Web site contains information on telephone and internet scams. You can also report fraud online. Special senior citizens page is also offered.

National Institute for Consumer Education
URL: http://emich.edu/public/coe/nice/nice.html
Site offers information on how to file a consumer complaint, how to report fraud, and what you need to know about finance, credit and comparison shopping.

Public Voice for Food and Health Policy
URL: http://www.publicvoice.org/pvoice.html
Web site features consumer information on pesticide reduction, nutrition labeling, seafood safety and inner-city food access.

The Self-Reliance Library
URL: http://whitehorse-research.com/m/m1.htm
The Self-Reliance Library contains a vast collection of internet resources, devoted to the broad subject of self-reliance. Site is organized into subject catagories which vary from consumer information and conspiracies to software and vegetarianism.

Victims of Credit Reporting
URL: http://pages.prodigy.com/ID/vcr/vcr.html
Site offers help for victims of inaccurate credit reporting. The nonprofit group that hosts this site lobbies for reform and posts educational information.

4

HELP FOR
THE CAR OWNER

Buying, servicing and selling a car involve such legal issues as negotiating contracts, purchasing auto insurance and pursuing legal remedies if things go wrong. This chapter lists resources that can help the car owner with these and related issues.

It begins with a list of major car manufacturers for those who want more information about a particular car on the market or who need to report a problem or register a complaint. Interested car buyers will also find web site addresses with lots of information, including free, no-hassle online auto purchasing services.

After spending hard-earned money on a car, the last thing you want to think about is having to get it fixed. But that's a reality for all car owners. Ideally, you'll get good, reasonably priced service. Unfortunately, what happens often falls short of the ideal.

According to the Council of Better Business Bureaus, 47,075 complaints were filed with its affiliates against auto repair shops in 1996. In actuality, the problem is even larger: in California alone, during the 1995-96 fiscal year, 28,030 complaints were filed with the Bureau of Automotive Repair in the State Department of Consumer Affairs.

If you own a new car and have a complaint with it, the first place to try to resolve your complaint is the local dealership where you bought the car. If your problem is not resolved there, contact the manufacturer's regional or national office (see Car Manufacturers Section). As always, it's a good idea to send copies of your letter to the public relations or customer service departments of the company, or both, because these offices tend to be more sensitive to customer opinions than those who deal daily in numbers and technology.

If you still cannot resolve your problem, contact one of the third-party dispute resolution programs listed in this section. If none of those works, contact your local or state consumer protection office (page 92) to determine if your state offers state-run dispute resolution programs.

If you suspect you have a vehicle problem that can be handled under your state's lemon law (all 50 states and the District of Columbia have them), call your local or state consumer protection office to ask about your rights. The Center for Auto Safety also can send you information about lemon laws (page 137).

Of course, you don't have to be a victim of fraudulent work and services. Your best defense is to educate yourself about your rights before you take your car in for repairs. Again, our web site list has a number of useful Internet addresses that can help you become an educated shopper of auto repair services. Many of them have material written by highly trained and certified mechanics.

CAR MANUFACTURERS

The list of car manufacturers is excerpted from the *1997 Consumer Resource Handbook,* published by the U.S. Office of Consumer Affairs.

ACURA

Customer Relations Department
Acura
1919 Torrance Blvd.
Torrance, CA 90501-2746
Toll free: 800-382-2238

ALFA-ROMEO DISTRIBUTORS OF NORTH AMERICA, INC.

Owner Relations Manager
Alfa-Romeo Distributors of North America, Inc.
6220 S. Orange Blossom Trail, Ste. 209
Orlando, FL 32809
Phone: 407-856-5000

AMERICAN HONDA MOTOR CO.

Corporate Office:
American Honda Motor Co., Inc.
Consumer Affairs Department
1919 Torrance Blvd.
Torrance, CA 90501-2746
Phone: 310-783-3260

For recall/campaign information, write or fax:
Customer Information Service
1919 Torrance Blvd.
Torrance, CA 90501-2746
Fax: 310-783-3785

California Customer Relations Department
American Honda Motor Co., Inc.
Western Zone
700 Van Ness Blvd.
Torrance, CA 90509-2260
Phone: 213-781-4565

Utah, Arizona, Colorado, New Mexico, Nebraska, Kansas, Oklahoma, Nevada, Texas (El Paso):
Customer Relations Department
American Honda Motor Co., Inc.
West Central Zone
1600 S. Abilene St., Ste. D
Aurora, CO 80012-5815
Phone: 303-696-3935

Maine, Vermont, New Hampshire, New York State (excluding NY City, its five boroughs, Long Island, Westchester County), Connecticut (excluding Fairfield County), Massachusetts, Rhode Island:
Customer Relations Department
American Honda Motor Co., Inc.
New England Zone
555 Old County Rd.
Windsor Locks, CT 06096-0465
Phone: 860-623-3310

Tennessee, Alabama, Georgia, Florida:
Customer Relations Department
American Honda Motor Co., Inc.
Southeastern Zone
1500 Morrison Pky.
Alpharetta, GA 30201-2199
Phone: 404-442-2045

Minnesota, Iowa, Missouri, Wisconsin, Illinois, Michigan (Upper Peninsula):
Customer Relations Department
American Honda Motor Co., Inc.
North Central Zone
601 Campus Dr., Ste. A-9
Arlington Heights, IL 60004-1407
Phone: 847-870-5600 (Honda automobiles only)

West Virginia, Maryland, Virginia,
North Carolina, South Carolina,
District of Columbia:
Customer Relations Department
American Honda Motor Co., Inc.
Mid-Atlantic Zone
902 Wind River Ln., Ste. 200
Gaithersburg, MD 20878-1974
Phone: 301-990-2020

Ohio (Steubenville), West Virginia
(Wheeling), Pennsylvania, New Jersey,
Delaware, New York (NY City, its five
boroughs, Long Island, Westchester
County), Connecticut (Fairfield
County):
Customer Relations Department
American Honda Motor Co., Inc.
Northeast Zone
115 Gaither Dr.
Moorestown, NJ 08057-0337
Phone: 609-235-5533

Michigan (except for Upper Peninsula),
Indiana, Ohio, Kentucky:
Customer Relations Department
American Honda Motor Co., Inc.
Central Zone
101 S. Stanfield Rd.
Troy, OH 45373-8010
Phone: 513-332-6250

Washington, Oregon, Idaho, Montana,
Wyoming, North Dakota, South Dakota,
Hawaii, Alaska:
Customer Relations Department
American Honda Motor Co., Inc.
Northwest Zone
12439 N.E. Airport Way
Portland, OR 97220-0186
Phone: 503-256-0943

Texas (excluding El Paso), Arkansas
(excluding Fayetteville, Bentonville,
Fort Smith, Jonesboro), Oklahoma
(Lawton, Ardmore), Louisiana,
Mississippi:

Customer Relations Department
American Honda Motor Co., Inc.
South Central Zone
4529 Royal Ln.
Irving, TX 75063-2583
Phone: 214-929-5481

AMERICAN ISUZU MOTORS, INC.

Headquarters:
American Isuzu Motors, Inc.
Customer Relations Department
2300 Pellisier Pl.
P.O. Box 995
Whittier, CA 90608
Phone: 310-699-0500
Toll free: 800-255-6727

California, Alaska, Hawaii, Idaho (north-
ern), Nevada, Oregon, Washington:
Regional Customer Relations Manager
American Isuzu Motors, Inc.
One Autry St.
Irvine, CA 92718-2785
Phone: 714-770-2626

Alabama, Florida, Georgia, Mississippi,
North Carolina, South Carolina:
Regional Customer Relations Manager
American Isuzu Motors, Inc.
Southeastern Region
205 Hembree Park Dr.
P.O. Box 6250
Roswell, GA 30076
Phone: 404-475-1995

Illinois, Indiana, Iowa, Michigan,
Minnesota, Missouri (except Kansas
City Metro Area), North Dakota, Ohio,
Wisconsin, South Dakota, Nebraska:
Regional Customer Relations Manager
American Isuzu Motors, Inc.
Central Region
695 Tollgate Rd.
Elgin, IL 60123
Phone: 847-931-8050

Connecticut, Maine, Massachusetts, New Hampshire, New Jersey (north of Toms River), New York, Rhode Island, Vermont:
Regional Customer Relations Manager
American Isuzu Motors, Inc.
Northeast Region
3 Stewart Ct.
P.O. Box 3015
Denville, NJ 07834
Phone: 201-328-3000

Arizona, Arkansas, Kansas (Kansas City Metro Area), Louisiana, Nevada (southern), New Mexico, Oklahoma, Texas, Colorado, Wyoming, Utah, Montana, Idaho (southern), Missouri (Kansas City Metro area):
Regional Customer Relations Manager
American Isuzu Motors, Inc.
Southwest Region
1150 Isuzu Pky.
Grand Prairie, TX 75050
Phone: 214-647-2911

New Jersey (south of Toms River), Pennsylvania, Maryland, Delaware, Kentucky, Tennessee, Virginia, West Virginia:
Regional Customer Relations Manager
American Isuzu Motors, Inc.
1 Isuzu Way
Glen Burnie, MD 21061
Phone: 410-761-2121

AMERICAN MOTORS CORP.
SEE CHRYSLER CORP. ZONE AND CORPORATE OFFICES

AMERICAN SUZUKI MOTOR CORP.

P.O. Box 1100
Brea, CA 92822-1100
Attn: Customer Relations Department
Phone: 714-996-7040, ext. 380 (motorcycles)
Toll free: 800-934-0934 (automotive only)

AUDI OF AMERICA, INC.

Customer Relations
Audi of America, Inc.
3800 Hamlin Road
Auburn Hills, MI 48326
Toll free: 800-822-2834 (general assistance and customer relations)
Toll free: 800-955-5100 (replacement and repurchase assistance)

BMW OF NORTH AMERICA, INC.

Corporate Office:
National Customer Relations Manager
BMW of North America, Inc.
P.O. Box 1227
Westwood, NJ 07675-1227
Toll free: 800-831-1117

CHRYSLER CORPORATION

Corporate Office:
Chrysler Customer Center
Chrysler Corp.
P.O. Box 21-8004
Auburn Hills, MI 48321-8004
Toll free: 800-992-1997
Toll free: 800-763-8422

Phoenix Zone Office
Customer Relations Manager
Chrysler Corp.
11811 N. Tatum Blvd., Ste. 4025
Phoenix, AZ 85028-1627
Phone: 602-494-6820

Los Angeles Zone Office
Customer Relations Manager
Chrysler Corp.
7700 Irvine Center Dr., 3rd Fl.
Irvine, CA 92618-2924
Phone: 714-450-5200
Toll free: 800-207-3025

San Francisco Zone Office
Customer Relations Manager
Chrysler Corp.
6150 Stoneridge Mall Rd., Ste. 200
P.O. Box 5009
Pleasanton, CA 94566-0509
Toll free: 800-987-9809

Denver Zone Office
Customer Relations Manager
Chrysler Corp.
12225 E. 39th Ave.
Denver, CO 80239
Phone: 303-373-8888

Orlando Zone Office
Customer Relations Manager
Chrysler Corp.
8000 S. Orange Blossom Trail
Orlando, FL 32809
Phone: 407-888-5430

Chicago Zone Office
Customer Relations Manager
Chrysler Corp.
650 Warrenville Rd., Ste. 502
Lisle, IL 60532
Phone: 630-515-2450

Kansas City Zone Office
Customer Relations Manager
Chrysler Corp.
P.O. Box 25745
Overland Park, KS 66225-5745
Phone: 913-469-3000

New Orleans Zone Office
Customer Relations Manager
Chrysler Corp.
1 Galleria Blvd.
Metairie, LA 70004
Phone: 504-833-4800

Washington, D.C. Zone Office
Customer Relations Manager
Chrysler Corp.
P.O. Box 1900
Bowie, MD 20717-1900
Phone: 301-464-4000
Toll free: 800-763-8422

Minneapolis Zone Office
Customer Relations Manager
Chrysler Corp.
13005 Highway 55
Minneapolis, MN 55441-3805
Phone: 612-553-2546

Syracuse Zone Office
Customer Relations Manager
Chrysler Corp.
5788 Widewater Pky.
Dewitt, NY 13214-0603
Phone: 315-445-6954

New York Zone Office
Customer Relations Manager
Chrysler Corp.
500 Route 303
Tappan, NY 10983-1592
Phone: 914-578-2221

Portland Zone Office
Customer Relations Manager
Chrysler Corp.
10030 S.W. Allen Blvd.
Beaverton, OR 97005
Phone: 503-526-5555

Philadelphia Zone Office
Customer Relations Manager
Chrysler Corp.
Valley Brook Corporate Center
101 Lindenwood Dr.
Malvern, PA 19355-0725
Phone: 610-251-2990

Pittsburgh Zone Office
Customer Relations Manager
Chrysler Corp.
Penn Center West 3, Ste. 420
Pittsburgh, PA 15276-0198
Phone: 412-788-7070

Memphis Zone Office
Customer Relations Manager
Chrysler Corp.
P.O. Box 18050
Memphis, TN 38181-0050
Phone: 901-797-3870

Dallas Zone Office
Customer Relations Manager
Chrysler Corp.
P.O. Box 110162
Carrollton, TX 75011-0162
Phone: 214-418-4600

Houston Zone Office
Customer Relations Manager
Chrysler Corp.
363 N. Sam Houston Pkwy., East
Ste. 590
Houston, TX 77060-2404
Phone: 713-820-7067

Milwaukee Zone Office
Customer Relations Manager
Chrysler Corp.
20935 Swenson Dr., Ste. 400
P.O. Box 1634
Waukesha, WI 53187-1634
Phone: 414-798-3750

DAIHATSU AMERICA, INC.

4422 Corporate Center Dr.
Los Alamitos, CA 90720
Toll free: 800-777-7070

FERRARI NORTH AMERICA, INC.

Corporate Office:
Umberto Masoni
Director of Service and Parts
Ferrari North America, Inc.
250 Sylvan Ave.
Englewood Cliffs, NJ 07632
Phone: 201-816-2684

FORD MOTOR CO.

Customer Relations Manager
Ford Motor Co.
300 Renaissance Center
P.O. Box 43360
Detroit, MI 48243
Toll free: 800-392-3673 (all makes)
Toll free: 800-521-4140 (Lincoln and Mercury only)

Toll free: 800-241-3673 (towing and dealer location service)
TDD Toll free: 800-232-5952

GENERAL MOTORS CORP.

Customer Assistance Center
Chevrolet/Geo Motor Division
General Motors Corp.
P.O. Box 7047
Troy, MI 48007-7047
Toll free: 800-222-1020
TDD Toll free: 800-TDD-CHEV
Toll free: 800-243-8872
(roadside assistance)

Customer Assistance Center
Pontiac Division
General Motors Corp.
1 Pontiac Plaza
Pontiac, MI 48340-2952
Toll free: 800-762-2737
TDD Toll free: 800-TDD-PONT

Customer Assistance Network
Oldsmobile Division
General Motors Corp.
P.O. Box 30095
Lansing, MI 48909-7595
Toll free: 800-442-6537
TDD Toll free: 800-TDD-OLDS

Customer Assistance Center
Buick Motor Division
General Motors Corp.
902 E. Hamilton Ave.
Flint, MI 48550
Toll free: 800-521-7300
TDD Toll free: 800-832-8425

Consumer Assistance Center
Cadillac Motor Car Division
General Motors Corp.
P.O. Box 9025
Warren, MI 48090-9025
Toll free: 800-458-8006
TDD Toll free: 800-TDD-CMCC

Consumer Assistance Center
GMC Truck Division
General Motors Corp.
31 Judson St.
Pontiac, MI 48342-2230
Toll free: 800-462-8782
TDD Toll free: 800-462-8583

Saturn Assistance Center
Saturn Corp.
General Motors Corp.
100 Saturn Pky.
Spring Hill, TN 37174
Toll free: 800-553-6000
TDD Toll free: 800-TDD-6000

HONDA
SEE AMERICAN HONDA MOTOR CO.,
INC.

HYUNDAI MOTOR AMERICA

Consumer Affairs
Hyundai Motor America
10550 Talbert Ave.
P.O. Box 20850
Fountain Valley, CA 92728-0850
Toll free: 800-633-5151

ISUZU
SEE AMERICAN ISUZU MOTORS, INC.

JAGUAR CARS INC.

U.S. National Headquarters:
Customer Relations Department
Jaguar Cars Inc.
555 MacArthur Blvd.
Mahwah, NJ 07430-2327
Phone: 201-818-8500
Toll free: 800-452-4827

JEEP/EAGLE DIVISION OF
CHRYSLER CORP.
SEE CHRYSLER CORP. ZONE AND
CORPORATE OFFICES

KIA MOTOR AMERICA, INC.

Owner Relations Manager
6220 S. Orange Blossom Trail, Ste. 209
Orlando, FL 32809
Phone: 407-856-5000

MAZDA MOTOR OF AMERICA,
INC.

Corporate Headquarters:
Customer Relations Manager
Mazda Motor of America, Inc.
P.O. Box 19734
Irvine, CA 92713-9734
Toll free: 800-222-5500

MERCEDES BENZ OF NORTH
AMERICA, INC.

Customer Assistance Center
1 Glenview Rd.
Montvale, NJ 07645
Toll free: 800-222-0100
Toll free: 800-367-6372 (800-FOR-
MERC)

MITSUBISHI MOTOR SALES OF
AMERICA, INC.

Corporate Office:
Attn.: Customer Relations
National Consumer Relations Manager
Mitsubishi Motor Sales of America, Inc.
6400 W. Katella Ave.
Cypress, CA 90630-0064
Toll free: 800-222-0037

NISSAN MOTOR CORP. IN USA

Nissan Motor Corp. in USA
P.0. Box 191
Gardena, CA 90248-0191
Toll free: 800-647-7261 (all consumer
inquiries)

PEUGEOT MOTORS OF AMERICA, INC.

William J. Atanasio
National Customer Relations Manager
Peugeot Motors of America, Inc.
P.O. Box 607
1 Peugeot Plaza
Lyndhurst, NJ 07071-3498
Phone: 201-935-8400
Toll free: 800-345-5549

PORSCHE CARS NORTH AMERICA

Manager, Owner Relations
Porsche Cars North America, Inc.
100 W. Liberty St.
P.O. Box 30911
Reno, NV 89520-3911
Toll free: 800-545-8039

SAAB CARS USA, INC.

Customer Assistance Center
Saab Cars USA, Inc.
4405-A Saab Dr.
P.O. Box 9000
Norcross, GA 30091
Toll free: 800-955-9007

SUBARU OF AMERICA, INC.

National Customer Service Center
Subaru of America, Inc.
Subaru Plaza
P.O. Box 6000
Cherry Hill, NJ 08034-6000
Toll free: 800-782-2783

HAWAII SCHUMAN CARRIAGE CO.

1234 S. Beretania Street
P.O. Box 2420
Honolulu, HI 96804
Phone: 808-553-6211

SUZUKI
SEE AMERICAN SUZUKI MOTOR CORP.

TOYOTA MOTOR SALES, INC.

Customer Assistance Center
Toyota Motor Sales USA, Inc.
Department A102 19001
S. Western Ave.
Torrance, CA 90509-2991
Toll free: 800-331-4331
TDD Toll free: 800-443-4999
Fax: 310-618-7814

VOLKSWAGEN

Customer Relations
Volkswagen United States, Inc.
3800 Hamlin Rd.
Auburn Hills, MI 48326
Toll free: 800-822-8987 (general assistance and customer relations)

VOLVO CARS OF NORTH AMERICA

Corporate Office:
Customer Service
Volvo Cars of North America
P.O. Box 914
Rockleigh, NJ 07647-0914
Phone: 201-767-4760
Toll free: 800-458-1552

RESOLVING PROBLEMS

Auto Arbitration Programs

Check with your state's consumer protection office (Chapter 3) to see if your state offers a state-run dispute resolution program for auto-related problems. For a regional office in your area that offers an automotive arbitration program, you can also contact:

Automotive Consumer Action Program (AUTOCAP)
8400 Westpark Dr.
McLean, VA 22102
Phone: 703-821-7144

BBB'S Auto Line
Council of Better Business Bureaus, Inc.
4200 Wilson Blvd., Ste. 800
Arlington, VA 22203-1804
Toll free: 800-955-5100

Chrysler Corporation
Chrysler Customer Center
P.O. Box 21-8004
Auburn Hills, MI 48321-8004
Toll free: 800-992-1997

Ford Dispute Settlement Board
P.O. Box 5120
Southfield, MI 48086-5120
Toll free: 800-392-3673

Auto Saftey Problems

If you have a safety problem with your vehicle, or want to obtain recall and crash test information, you can call the National Highway Traffic Safety Administration. For additional information on auto safety, or to obtain a copy of *The Car Book 1997: The Definitive Buyer's Guide to Car Safety, Fuel Economy, Maintenance, and Much More,* by Jack Gillis, call or write The Center for Auto Safety.

National Highway Traffic Safety Administration
Washington, DC 20590
Phone: 202-366-0123
Toll free: 800-424-9393
(Auto Safety Hotline)

The Center for Auto Safety
2001 S St., NW, Ste. 410
Washington, DC 20009
Phone: 202-328-7700

Lemon Laws

All 50 states and the District of Columbia have a new car "lemon law" that allows the owner a refund or replacement when a new vehicle has a substantial problem that is not fixed within a reasonable number of attempts. For a review of your state's lemon laws, write to group above and request *Lemon Law Summary*. Include a self-addressed stamped (55 cents) envelope.

The Center for Auto Safety
2001 S St., NW, Ste. 410
Washington, DC 20009
Phone: 202-328-7700

WEB SITES

ON CAR PURCHASING

Auto-By-Tel
URL: http://www.autobytel.com/
Buy, sell or lease autos online through this free service. Auto-By-Tel can also obtain low-cost auto insurance and financing for its customers.

CarSmart
URL: http://www.carsmart.com/
A free service for finding new and used vehicles, price quotes, links to auto manufacturers.

Consumer Reports Auto Insurance Price Service
URL: http://www.consumerinsure.org/
Consumer Reports' exclusive database compares the policies in 8 states of as many as 70 insurance policies based on the information you provide.

Edmunds
URL: http://www.edmunds.com/
Tons of good, free information for anyone buying a new or used car, including price comparisons, MSRPs, and more.

Internet AutoSource
URL: http://www.autosource-usa.com/
Reviews of makes and models and information for finding a dealer.

America Online and CompuServe customers can access lots of good information about buying and selling cars through Consumer Reports Magazine by using the keyword "consumer" for America Online and "go consumer" for CompuServe.

ON CAR REPAIR

Autobody Web
URL: http://www.autobodyweb.com/
Searchable online database of over 60,000 autobody shops in North America.

AutoShop Online
URL: http://www.autoshop-online.com/
Advice from the experts on the repair, maintenance and operation of your car.

Boston-Area Auto Mechanics
URL: http://www.osf.org/~bowe/bbn-auto/
A rated review list of regional auto mechanics in Boston, Massachusetts.

The Car Guy
URL: http://www.thecarguy.com/
Site hosted by nationally certified ASE Advanced Level Technician, auto journalist and consumer advisor. Site offers helpful tips, news and informaton on cars.

Car Talk
URL: http://cartalk.msn.com/
Advice, information and resouces from National Public Radio's famous brother mechanics, Tom and Ray Magliozzi.

Family Car
URL: http://www.familycar.com/
Consumer information on purchasing a new or used car, maintaining it, finding a repair shop and dealing with your mechanic.

Web Garage
URL: http://webgarage.com/ci/index.htm
A library of information about car repair. Links to other auto-related web sites, including dealers, products and services, car magazines and consumer information.

CONSUMER ORGANIZATIONS

Car Care Council
URL: http://www.carcarecouncil.org/
A non-profit group that educates motorists, free-of-charge, about the benefits of proper vehicle maintenance.

BBB AUTOLINE
URL: http://www.bbb.org/complaints/BBBautoLine.html
Information on how the program works, kinds of disputes handled and who to contact.

5

HELP RESOLVING
LAWYER COMPLAINTS

Every state has a lawyer-run agency that processes consumer complaints against lawyers. In about one-third of the states, these agencies are run directly by state bar associations. Their only function is to police violations of the state's rules of professional conduct, based on a model written by the American Bar Association. In the remaining states, programs are run by each state's highest court.

Unfortunately, the attorney discipline system is riddled with flaws. More than 100,000 complaints against lawyers are filed each year with these agencies, but only about 2 percent of them result in anything more than a private reprimand. Even so, it is important that clients who encounter problems file complaints with these agencies, if only to document that problems do occur and need to be addressed. Some states have toll free numbers to make it easier for clients to complain.

Although these agencies cannot compensate you for the problems your lawyer caused, they can impose one of four different levels of discipline: private reprimand, public reprimand, suspension and disbarment.

A client who thinks his or her lawyer has over-billed for services or has stolen money should contact the state bar's fee arbitration or client security trust fund program. This section of the chapter includes the addresses and telephone numbers for grievance committees, client security fund offices and fee arbitration programs for all 50 states, the District of Columbia, the Virgin Islands and Puerto Rico. Where state offices handle these matters, that office is listed. If the issue is handled at a local office, that office is either listed or we suggest you contact the state office for a local referral. Some state bar associations (10 as of this printing) have web sites with links to information on how their discipline complaint systems works. Some even provide downloadable forms.

For consumers of legal services, one of the more exciting things to happen on the Internet is its use to inform prospective clients about their lawyer's prior complaint record. The current lawyer-run system keeps this information confidential and, in some jurisdictions, even threatens consumers with jail time if they divulge information about having filed a complaint against a lawyer.

Although in their infant stages, a few web sites (which HALT anticipates will grow) have begun to appear with the intent of lifting the curtain that now conceals attorney discipline proceedings and findings from public view. They are listed at the end of this section.

STATE BAR PROGRAMS

Data on grievance committees and client security fund offices were compiled by the American Bar Association in 1996. Fee arbitration program data were compiled by HALT in the Spring of 1997. Because the names and addresses of state agencies may change at any time, you should verify the information with your state bar or the American Bar Association.

ALABAMA

Attorney Grievance
General Counsel
Alabama State Bar
Center for Professional Responsibility
415 Dexter Ave.
P.O. Box 671
Montgomery, AL 36104
Phone: 205-269-1515
Fax: 205-261-6311

Client Security Fund
Claims Administrator
P.O. Box 671
Montgomery, AL 36101
Phone: 334-269-1515
Fax: 334-361-6311

Fee Arbitration
Voluntary arbitration
No statewide program, state bar refers cases to local fee arbitration where available.
(Address, telephone same as Client Security Fund.)

ALASK

Attorney Grievance
Bar Counsel
Alaska Bar Association
510 L St., Ste. 602
P.O. Box 100279
Anchorage, AK 99510-0279
Phone: 907-272-7469
Fax: 907-272-2932

Client Security Fund
Alaska Bar Association
(Address, phone, and fax same as Attorney Grievance.)

Fee Arbitration
Mandatory arbitration
Alaska Bar Association
Fee Arbitration Program
Coordinator: Stephan Van Goor
(Address, phone, fax same as Attorney Grievance.)

ARIZONA

Attorney Grievance
Chief Bar Counsel
State Bar of Arizona
111 W. Monroe, Ste. 1800
Phoenix, AZ 85003-1742
Phone: 602-340-7241
Fax: 602-271-4930

Client Security Fund
Special Services Counsel
(Address, fax same as Attorney Grievance.)
Phone: 602-340-7284

Fee Arbitration
Voluntary arbitration
State Bar of Arizona
Fee Arbitration Program
Coordinator: Diana Kehayes
Phone: 602-340-7285
(Address, fax same as Attorney Grievance.)

ARKANSAS

Attorney Grievance
Supreme Court of Arkansas
Committee on Professional Conduct
Justice Bldg.
625 Marshall St.
Little Rock, AR 72201
Phone: 501-376-0313
Fax: 501-374-1853

Client Security Fund
Senior Staff Attorney
Committee on Professional Conduct
Justice Bldg., Rm. 205
625 Marshall St.
Little Rock, AR 72201
Phone: 501-376-0313
Fax: 501-374-1853

Fee Arbitration
None.

CALIFORNIA

Attorney Grievance
Chief Trial Counsel
State Bar of California
Office of the Chief Trial Counsel
1149 S. Hill St., 10th Fl.
Los Angeles, CA 90015
Phone: 213-765-1000
Toll free: 800-843-9053 (In-state only)
Fax: 213-765-1029

Client Security Fund
State Bar of California
1149 S. Hill St., 7th Fl.
Los Angeles, CA 90015
Phone: 213-765-1161
Fax: 213-765-1158

Fee Arbitration
State Bar of California
Mandatory Fee Arbitration
100 Van Ness Ave., 28th Fl.
San Francisco, CA 94102-5238
Phone: 415-241-2020

COLORADO

Attorney Grievance
Colorado Supreme Court
Office of the Disciplinary Counsel
Dominion Plaza Bldg.
600 17th St., Ste. 510 S.
Denver, CO 80202-5435
Phone: 303-893-8121
Fax: 303-893-5302

Client Security Fund
None

Fee Arbitration
Voluntary arbitration
Legal Fee Arbitration Committee
Coordinator: Julia Webb
1900 Grant St., Ste. 900
Denver, CO 80203
Phone: 303-860-1112
Toll free: 800-332-6736 (In-state only)
Fax: 303-894-0821

CONNECTICUT

Attorney Grievance
Statewide Grievance Committee
287 Main St., 2nd Fl., Ste. 2
East Hartford, CT 06118-1885
Phone: 860-568-5157

Client Security Fund
Public Service Manager
Connecticut Bar Association
101 Corporate Pl.
Rocky Hill, CT 06067-1894
Phone: 860-721-0025
Fax: 860-257-4125

Fee Arbitration
Voluntary arbitration
Arbitration of Legal Fee Disputes
Coordinator: Margie Roldan
(Address, phone, fax same as
Client Security Fund.)

DELAWARE

Attorney Grievance
Office of Disciplinary
Counsel
200 W. 9th St., Ste. 300A
P.O. Box 472
Wilmington, DE 19899
Phone: 302-571-8703
Fax: 302-571-9433

Client Security Fund
Administrator
Delaware State Bar Association
200 W. 9th St., Ste. 300-B
Wilmington, DE 19801
Phone: 302-652-2117
Fax: 302-658-4605

Fee Arbitration
Vouluntary arbitration
Fee Dispute Conciliation
and Mediation Committee
P.O. Box 2328
Wilmington, DE 19899
Phone: 302-655-2599

DISTRICT OF COLUMBIA

Attorney Grievance
District Office:
Board on Professional Responsibility
District of Columbia
515 5th St., NW, Bldg. A, Rm. 127
Washington, DC 20001-2797
Phone: 202-638-1501
Fax: 202-638-0862

Client Security Fund
Administrator
District of Columbia Bar
Client Security Bar
1250 H St., NW, Ste. 6000
Washington, DC 20005-3908
Phone: 202-626-3437
Fax: 202-626-3471

Fee Arbitration
Mandatory arbitration
Attorney-Client Arbitration Board
Director: Carla Freudenburg
Phone: 202-737-4700
(Address, fax same as
Client Security Fund.)

FLORIDA

Attorney Grievance
Staff Counsel
The Florida Bar
650 Apalachee Pkwy.
Tallahassee, FL 32399-2300
Toll free: 800-342-8060 (FL only)
Toll free: 800-874-0005 (Out-of-State)
Fax: 904-561-5665

Client Security Fund
Clients' Security Fund Coordinator
Phone: 904-561-5812
Fax: 904-561-5827
(Address same as Attorney Grievance.)

Fee Arbitration
Voluntary arbitration
Fee Arbitration Committee
(Address, telephone same as
Attorney Grievance.)

GEORGIA

Attorney Grievance
General Counsel
State Bar of Georgia
800 The Hurt Bldg.
50 Hurt Plaza
Atlanta, GA 30303-2934
Phone: 404-527-8720
Fax: 404-527-8717

Client Security Fund
Assistant General Counsel
(Address, telephone same as
Attorney Grievance.)
Fax: 404-527-8744

Fee Arbitration
Voluntary arbitration
Fee Arbitration Program
Coordinator: Rita Payne
(Address, phone, fax same as
Attorney Grievance.)
Toll free: 800-334-6865

HAWAII

Attorney Grievance
Chief Disciplinary Counsel
Office of Disciplinary Counsel
Supreme Court of Hawaii
1164 Bishop St., Ste. 600
Honolulu, HI 96813
Phone: 808-521-4591
Fax: 808-545-2719

Client Security Fund
Acting Fund Administrator
Lawyers' Fund for Client Protection
Phone: 808-599-2483
(Address, fax same as
Attorney Grievance.)

Fee Arbitration
Voluntary arbitration
Attorney-Client Coordination
Committee
Hawaii State Bar Association
1136 Union Mall, PH-1
Honolulu, HI 96813
Phone: 808-537-1868

IDAHO

Attorney Grievance
Bar Counsel
Idaho State Bar
P.O. Box 895
525 W. Jefferson
Boise, ID 83701-0895
Phone: 208-334-4500
Fax: 208-334-4515

Client Security Fund
Executive Director
(Address, phone, fax same as
Attorney Grievance.)

Fee Arbitration
Voluntary arbitration
Fee Arbitration Program
Coordinator: Linda Pruitte
(Address, phone, fax same as
Attorney Grievance.)

ILLINOIS

Attorney Grievance
Attorney Registration and
Disciplinary Commission of the
Supreme Court of Illinois
1 Prudential Plaza
130 E. Randolph Dr., Ste. 1500
Chicago, IL 60601
Phone: 312-565-2600
Fax: 312-565-2320
Toll free: 800-826-8625 (In-State only)

Client Security Fund
Client Protection Counsel
(Address, phone, fax same as
Attorney Grievance.)

Fee Arbitration
Voluntary arbitration
Illinois State Bar Association
20 S. Clark St., Ste. 900
Chicago, IL 60603
Phone: 312-726-8775

INDIANA

Attorney Grievance
Executive Secretary
Indiana Supreme Court
Disciplinary Commission
1150 W. Market St., Ste.1060
Indianapolis, IN 46204-3417
Phone: 317-232-1807
Fax: 317-232-0261

Client Security Fund
Executive Director
Indiana State Bar Association
Clients' Financial Assistance Fund
230 E. Ohio St., 4th Fl.
Indianapolis, IN 46204
Phone: 317-639-5465
Fax: 317-266-2588

Fee Arbitration
Voluntary arbitration
No statewide program, state bar refers
cases to local fee arbitration where
available.
(Address, telephone, fax same as
Client Security Fund.)

IOWA

Attorney Grievance
Ethics Administrator
Iowa State Bar Association
Committee on Professional
Ethics & Conduct
521 E. Locust St., 3rd Fl.
Des Moines, IA 50309-1939
Phone: 515-243-0027
Fax: 515-243-2511

Client Security Fund
Administrator
Client Security & Attorney
Disciplinary Commission
State Capitol
Des Moines, IA 50319
Phone: 515-246-8076
Fax: 515-246-8059

Fee Arbitration
Voluntary arbitration
No statewide program, state bar refers
cases to local fee arbitration where
available.
(Address, telephone, fax same as
Attorney Grievance.)

KANSAS

Attorney Grievance
Disciplinary Administrator
Supreme Court of Kansas
3706 SW Topeka Blvd., Ste. 100
Topeka, KS 66609-1239
Phone: 913-296-2486
Fax: 913-296-6049

Client Security Fund
Clerk of the Supreme Court
Kansas Lawyers' Fund
for Client Protection
Kansas Judicial Center
301 SW 10th Ave., Rm. 374
Topeka, KS 66612-1507
Phone: 913-296-3229
Fax: 913-296-1028

Fee Arbitration
Voluntary arbitration
Fee Dispute Committee
Coordinator: Judge Robert Fairchild
1200 Harrison
Topeka, KS
Phone: 785-234-5696
Fax: 785-234-3813

KENTUCKY

Attorney Grievance
Bar Counsel
Kentucky Bar Association
Kentucky Bar Center
514 W. Main St.
Frankfort, KY 40601-1883
Phone: 502-564-3795
Fax: 502-564-3225

Client Security Fund
(Address, phone, fax same as
Attorney Grievance.)

Fee Arbitration
Voluntary arbitration
Legal Fee Arbitration Plan
(Address, telephone, fax same as
Attorney Grievance.)

LOUISIANA

Attorney Grievance
Chief Disciplinary Counsel
Office of the Disciplinary Board
Louisiana State Bar Association
4000 S. Sherwood Forest Blvd., Ste. 607
Baton Rouge, LA 70816
Phone: 504-293-3900
Fax: 504-293-3300

Client Security Fund
Staff Liaison
Louisiana State Bar Association
601 St. Charles Ave.
New Orleans, LA 70130
Phone: 504-566-1600
Fax: 504-528-9154

Fee Arbitration
Voluntary arbitration
Lawyer Dispute Resolution Program
(Address, telephone, same as
Client Security Fund.)
Fax: 504-566-0930

MAINE

Attorney Grievance
Bar Counsel
Maine Board of Overseers of the Bar
97 Winthrop St.
P.O. Box 1820
Augusta, ME 04332-1820
Phone: 207-623-1121
Fax: 207-623-4175

Client Security Fund
None (Considering a new fund,
committee formed to study issue).

Fee Arbitration
Mandatory arbitration
Fee Arbitration Commission
Coordinator: Valerie Stanfill, Esq.
(Address, phone, fax same as
Attorney Grievance.)

MARYLAND

Attorney Grievance
Bar Counsel
Attorney Grievance Commission
100 Community Pl., Ste. 3301
Crownsville, MD 21032-2027
Phone: 410-514-7051
Fax: 410-987-4690

Client Security Fund
Administrator
208 Calvert St.
Salisbury, MD 21801-2804
Phone: 410-543-8410
Fax: 401-749-7509

Fee Arbitration
Mandatory arbitration
Committee on Resolution
of Fee Disputes
520 Fayette St.
Baltimore, MD 21201
Phone: 410-685-7878

MASSACHUSETTS

Attorney Grievance
Office of the Bar Counsel
Massachusetts Board of Bar Overseers
75 Federal St., 7th Fl.
Boston, MA 02110
Phone: 617-357-1860
Fax: 617-357-1872

Client Security Fund
Assistant Board Counsel
(Address, fax same as
Attorney Grievance.)
Phone: 617-357-1860 ext. 50

Fee Arbitration
Voluntary arbitration
Legal Fee Arbitration Board
Massachusetts Bar Association
Coordinator: Stacy Shunk, Esq.
20 West St.
Boston, MA 02111
Phone: 617-338-0500
Fax: 617-338-0636

MICHIGAN

Attorney Grievance
State Office:
Grievance Administrator
Attorney Grievance Commission
Marquette Bldg., Ste. 256
243 W. Congress
Detroit, MI 48226
Phone: 313-961-6585
Fax: 313-961-5819
Toll free: (800) 968-1442

Client Security Fund
Assistant Counsel
State Bar of Michigan
Michael Franck Bldg.
310 Townsend St.
Lansing, MI 48933
Phone: 517-372-9033, ext. 3010
Fax: 517-482-6248

Fee Arbitration
Voluntary arbitration
Fee Arbitration Program
306 Townsend St.
Lansing, MI 48933-2083
Phone: 517-346-6300
Fax: 517-482-6248

MINNESOTA

Attorney Grievance
Director
Office of Professional Responsibility
25 Constitution Ave., Ste. 105
St. Paul, MN 55155-1500
Phone: 612-296-3952
Toll free: 800-657-3601 (Out-of-State)
Fax: 612-297-5801

Client Security Fund
Minnesota Judicial Center
(Address, phone, fax same as Attorney
Grievance.)

Fee Arbitration
Voluntary arbitration
No statewide program, disciplinary committee refers cases to local fee arbitration where available.
(Address, telephone same as
Attorney Grievance.)

MISSISSIPPI

Attorney Grievance
General Counsel
Mississippi State Bar
643 N. State St.
P.O. Box 2168
Jackson, MS 39225-2168
Phone: 601-948-4471
Fax: 601-355-8635

Client Security Fund
Assistant General Counsel
Mississippi State Bar
(Address, phone, fax same as
Attorney Grievance.)

Fee Arbitration
Voluntary arbitration
Resolution of Fee Disputes Committee
Coordinator: Michael Martz
(Address, phone, fax same as
Attorney Grievance.)

MISSOURI

Attorney Grievance
Office of Chief Disciplinary Counsel
Missouri Supreme Court
3335 America Ave.
Jefferson City, MO 65109
Phone: 314-635-7400
Fax: 314-635-2240

Client Security Fund
Administrator
P.O. Box 119
326 Monroe St.
Jefferson City, MO 65102
Phone: 314-635-4128
Fax: 314-659-8931

Fee Arbitration
Voluntary arbitration
No statewide program, state bar refers
cases to local fee arbitration
where available.
(Address, telephone, fax same as
Attorney Grievance.)

MONTANA

Attorney Grievance
Bar Counsel
State Bar of Montana
Commission on Practice of the
Supreme Court of Montana
P.O. Box 577
Helena, MT 59624
Phone: 406-442-7660
Fax: 406-442-7763

Client Security Fund
Executive Director
State Bar of Montana
(Address, phone, fax same as
Attorney Grievance.)

Fee Arbitration
Mandatory arbitration
State Bar of Montana
Fee Arbitration Program
Coordinator: G. Little
(Address, phone, fax same as
Attorney Grievance.)

NEBRASKA

Attorney Grievance
Counsel for Discipline
Nebraska State Bar Association
P.O. Box 81809
Lincoln, NE 68501
Phone: 402-475-7091
Fax: 402-475-7098

Client Security Fund
Administrator
Nebraska State Bar Association
635 S. 14th St.
Lincoln, NE 68501
(Address, fax, phone same as
Attorney Grievance).

Fee Arbitration
None.

NEVADA

Attorney Grievance
Bar Counsel
State Bar of Nevada
201 Las Vegas Blvd., Ste. 200
Las Vegas, NV 89101-6579
Phone: 702-382-2200
Fax: 702-385-2878

Client Security Fund
(Address same as Attorney Grievance.)
Toll free: 800-254-2797
Fax: 888-660-6767

Fee Arbitration
Voluntary Arbitration
Fee Dispute Arbitration Committee
Coordinator: Georgia Taylor
Toll free: 800-254-2797
(Address, phone, fax same as
Attorney Grievance.)

NEW HAMPSHIRE

Attorney Grievance
Administrator
New Hampshire Supreme Court
Professional Conduct Committee
4 Park St., Ste. 304
Concord, NH 03301
Phone: 603-224-5828

Client Security Fund
Administrator
Clients' Indemnity Fund
New Hampshire Bar Association
112 Pleasant St.
Concord, NH 03301
Phone: 603-224-6942
Fax: 603-224-2910

Fee Arbitration
Voluntary arbitration
Fee Dispute Resolution Committee
(Address, telephone, fax same as
Client Security Fund.)

NEW JERSEY

Attorney Grievance
Director, Office of Attorney Ethics
Supreme Court of New Jersey
Hughes Justice Complex, CN-963
25 W. Market St.
Trenton, NJ 08625
Phone: 609-530-4008
Fax: 609-530-4238

Client Security Fund
Director
New Jersey Lawyers' Fund
for Client Protection
Richard J. Hughes Justice Complex
P.O. 961
Trenton, NJ 08625-0961
Phone: 609-984-7179
Fax: 609-394-3637

Fee Arbitration
Mandatory arbitration
New Jersey Court
Fee Arbitration Program
Toll free: 800-406-8594 (in NJ only;
callers need to enter the 5-digit zip
code of where attorney practices to
get a referral).

NEW MEXICO

Attorney Grievance
Chief Disciplinary Counsel
Disciplinary Board of the Supreme
Court of New Mexico
400 Gold SW, Ste. 800
Albuquerque, NM 87102-3261
Phone: 505-842-5781
Fax: 505-766-6833

Client Security Fund
State Bar of New Mexico
P.O. Box 25883
Albuquerque, NM 87125
Phone: 505-797-6034
Fax: 505-828-3765

Fee Arbitration
Voluntary arbitration
Fee Arbitration Program
Coordinator: Maggie Coombos
Phone: 505-797-6000
Toll free: 800-876-6227
(Address, fax same as
Client Security Fund.)

NEW YORK

Attorney Grievance
In New York City: (First Dept.: Bronx,
New York County)
Chief Counsel
First Judicial Department
Departmental Disciplinary Committee
41 Madison Ave., 39th Fl.
New York, NY 10010
Phone: 212-685-1000
Fax: 212-545-8981

In New York City: (Second Dept.: Kings, Queens, Richmond Counties)
Chief Counsel
Second Judicial Department
2nd and 11th Judicial District
Grievance Committees
Municipal Bldg., 12th Fl.
210 Joralemon St.
Brooklyn, NY 11201
Phone: 718-624-7851
Fax: 718-643-9828

In New York State: (Second Dept.: Dutchess, Orange, Putnam, Rockland, and Westchester Counties)
Chief Counsel
Second Judicial Department
9th Judicial District
Grievance Committee
Crosswest Office Center
399 Knollwood Rd., Ste. 200
White Plains, NY 10603
Phone: 914-949-4540
Fax: 914-949-0997

In New York State: (Second Dept.: Nassau, Suffolk Counties)
Chief Counsel
New York State Grievance Committee
Tenth Judicial District- Second Dept.
6900 Jericho Tnpk., Ste. LL102
Syosset, NY 11791
Phone: 516-364-7344
Fax: 516-364-7355

In New York State: (Third Dept.)
Chief Attorney
Third Judicial Department Committee
on Professional Standards
Alfred E. Smith State Office Bldg., 22nd Fl.
P.O. Box 7013, Capitol Station Annex
Albany, NY 12225-0013
Phone: 518-474-8816
Fax: 518-474-0389

In New York State: (Fourth Dept., Fifth Dist.)
Chief Attorney
Fourth Judicial Dept.
5th District Grievance Committee
465 S. Salina St., Ste. 106
Syracuse, NY 13202
Phone: 315-471-1835
Fax: 315-479-0123

In New York State: (Fourth Dept., Seventh Dist.)
Chief Counsel
Fourth Judicial Dept.
7th District Grievance Committee
1002 Union Trust Bldg.
19 W. Main St.
Rochester, NY 14614
Phone: 716-546-8340
Fax: 716-546-6676

In New York State: (Fourth Dept., Eighth Dist.)
Chief Counsel
Fourth Judicial Dept.
8th District Grievance Committee
1036 Ellicott Square Bldg.
Buffalo, NY 14203
Phone: 716-858-1190
Fax: 716-856-2701

Client Security Fund
Assistant Counsel
Lawyer's Fund for Client Protection
55 Elk St.
Albany, NY 12210
Phone: 518-474-8438
Fax: 518-486-4178

Fee Arbitration
Voluntary arbitration
No statewide program, state bar refers cases to local fee arbitration where available.
New York State Bar
1 Elk St.
Albany, NY 12207
Phone: 518-463-3200

NORTH CAROLINA

Attorney Grievance
Counsel
North Carolina State Bar
208 Fayetteville St. Mall
P.O. Box 25908
Raleigh, NC 27611
Phone: 919-828-4620
Fax: 919-821-9168

Client Security Fund
Administrator
(Address, phone, fax same as
Attorney Grievance.)

Fee Arbitration
Mandatory arbitration
State Bar Fee Arbitration Program
Coordinator: Harry Warren
(Address, phone, fax same as
Attorney Grievance.)

NORTH DAKOTA

Attorney Grievance
Disciplinary Counsel
Disciplinary Board of the Supreme
Court of North Dakota
P.O. Box 2297
Bismarck, ND 58502-2297
Phone: 701-328-3925
Fax: 701-328-3964

Client Security Fund
Executive Director
North Dakota State Bar
515 1/2 E. Broadway, Ste. 101
Bismarck, ND 58502
Phone: 701-255-1404
Fax: 701-224-1621

Fee Arbitration
Voluntary arbitration
Arbitration of Fee Disputes
Coordinator: Tami Anderson
P.O. Box 2136
Bismarck, ND 58502
Phone: 701-255-1404
Toll free: 800-472-2685
Fax: 701-224-1621

OHIO

Attorney Grievance
Disciplinary Counsel
Office of Disciplinary Counsel of the
Supreme Court of Ohio
175 S. 3rd St., Ste. 280
Columbus, OH 43215-5134
Phone: 614-461-0256
Fax: 614-461-7205

In Akron: (*Summit County only*)
Executive Director
Akron Bar Association
90 S. High St.
Akron, OH 44308
Phone: 216-253-5007
Fax: 216-253-2140

In Cincinnati: (*Hamilton County only*)
Bar Counsel
Cincinnati Bar Association
35 E. 7th St., Ste. 800
Cincinnati, OH 45202-2411
Phone: 513-381-8213
Fax: 513-381-0528

In Cleveland: (*Cuyahoga County only*)
Counsel
Cleveland Bar Association
113 St. Clair Ave., NE, 2nd Fl.
Cleveland, OH 44114-1253
Phone: 216-696-3525
Fax: 216-696-2413

In Columbus: (*Franklin County only*)
Bar Counsel
Columbus Bar Association
175 S. 3rd St.
Columbus, OH 43215-5193
Phone: 614-225-6053
Fax: 614-221-4850

In Dayton: (*Montgomery County only*)
Executive Director
Dayton Bar Association
600 One 1st National Plaza
Dayton, OH 45402-1501
Phone: 513-222-7902
Fax: 513-222-1308

In Toledo: (*Lucas County only*)
Executive Director
Toledo Bar Association
311 N. Superior St.
Toledo, OH 43604
Phone: 419-242-9363
Fax: 419-242-3614

Client Security Fund
Administrator
Supreme Court of Ohio
Clients' Security Trust Fund
175 S. 3rd St., Ste. 285
Columbus, OH 43215-5134
Phone: 614-221-0562
Fax: 614-221-0638

Fee Arbitration
Voluntary arbitration
No statewide program, state bar refers
cases to local fee arbitration
where available.
Ohio State Bar Association
33 W. 11th Ave.
Columbus, OH 43201-2099
Phone: 614-487-2050

OKLAHOMA

Attorney Grievance
General Counsel
Oklahoma State Bar Association
1901 N. Lincoln Blvd.
P.O. Box 53036
Oklahoma City, OK 73152
Phone: 405-524-2365
Fax: 405-524-1115

Client Security Fund
Administrator
(Address, phone, fax same as
Attorney Grievance.)

Fee Arbitration
Mandatory arbitration
No statewide program, state bar refers
cases to local fee arbitration
where available.
(Address, telephone, fax same as
Attorney Grievance.)

OREGON

Attorney Grievance
Disciplinary Counsel
Oregon State Bar
P.O. Box 1689
5200 S.W. Meadows Rd.
Lake Oswego, OR 97035-0889
Phone: 503-620-0222
Fax: 503-684-1366

Client Security Fund
Administrator
Clients' Security Fund Committee
(Address, fax same as
Attorney Grievance.)
Phone: 503-620-0222, ext. 320

Fee Arbitration
Voluntary arbitration
Fee Arbitration Program
Coordinator: Sylvia Stevens
Phone: 503-620-0222, ext. 399
Toll free: 800-452-8260, ext. 399
Fax: 503-624-8326
(Address same as Attorney Grievance.)

PENNSYLVANIA

Attorney Grievance
Chief Disciplinary Counsel
The Disciplinary Board of the Supreme
Court of Pennsylvania
Union Trust Bldg., Ste. 400
501 Grant St.
Pittsburgh, PA 15219-4407
Phone: 412-565-3173
Fax: 412-565-7833

Client Security Fund
Executive Director
Pennsylvania Lawyers' Fund
for Client Security
5035 Ritter Rd., Ste. 900
Mechanicsburg, PA 17055
Toll free: 800-962-4618
Fax: 717-691-9005

Fee Arbitration
Voluntary arbitration
No statewide program, disciplinary
board refers cases to local fee arbitra-
tion where available.
(Address, telephone, fax same as
Attorney Grievance.)

PUERTO RICO

Attorney Grievance
Presidente
Comision de Etica Profesional
Colegio de Abogados de Puerto Rico
Apartado 1900
San Juan, PR 00902
Phone: 809-721-3358 or 723-6984
Fax: 809-725-0330

Client Security Fund
None.

Fee Arbitration
None.

RHODE ISLAND

Attorney Grievance
Chief Disciplinary Counsel
Disciplinary Board of the Supreme
Court of Rhode Island
Fogarty Judicial Annex
24 Weybasset St.
Providence, RI 02903
Phone: 401-277-3270
Fax: 401-277-1191

Client Security Fund
Ex-Officio
Rhode Island Bar Association
115 Cedar St.
Providence, RI 02903
Phone: 401-421-5740
Fax: 401-421-2703

Fee Arbitration
Voluntary arbitration
Fee Arbitration Committee
(Address, telephone, fax same as
Client Security Fund.)

SOUTH CAROLINA

Attorney Grievance
Administrative Assistant
Board of Commissioners
on Grievances and Discipline
P.O. Box 11330
Columbia, SC 29211
Phone: 803-734-2038

Client Security Fund
Administrator
South Carolina Bar
950 Taylor St.
P.O. Box 608
Columbia, SC 29202
Phone: 803-799-6653
Fax: 803-799-4118

Fee Arbitration
Mandatory arbitration
Resolution of Fee Disputes Board
Coordinator: Sarah Steen
(Address, phone, fax same as
Client Security Fund.)

SOUTH DAKOTA

Attorney Grievance
Counsel
State Bar of South Dakota
222 E. Capitol
Pierre, SD 57501-2596
Phone: 605-224-7554
Fax: 605-224-0282

Client Security Fund
Secretary-Treasurer
(Address, telephone, fax same as
Attorney Grievance.)

Fee Arbitration
None.

TENNESSEE

Attorney Grievance
Chief Disciplinary Counsel
Board of Professional Responsibility of
the Supreme Court of Tennessee
The Oaks Tower
1101 Kermit Dr., Ste. 730
Nashville, TN 37217
Phone: 615-361-7500
Fax: 615-367-2480

Client Security Fund
Executive Director
Tennessee Lawyers' Fund
for Client Protection
511 Union St., Ste. 1430
Nashville, TN 37219
Phone: 615-741-3097
Fax: 615-532-2477

Fee Arbitration
Voluntary arbitration
No statewide program, state bar refers
cases to local fee arbitration
where available.
(Address, telephone, fax same as
Client Security Fund.)

TEXAS

Attorney Grievance
General Counsel
State Bar of Texas
P.O. Box 12487
Austin, TX 78711
Toll free: 800-204-2222
Fax: 512-477-4607

Client Security Fund
Assistant General Counsel for
Corporate Affairs
(Address same as Attorney Grievance.)
Phone: 512-463-1463, ext. 2365
Fax: 512-473-2295

Fee arbitration
Voluntary arbitration
No statewide program, state bar refers
cases to local fee arbitration
where available.
(Address, telephone, fax same as
Attorney Grievance.)

UTAH

Attorney Grievance
Bar Counsel
Utah State Bar
Office of the Attorney Discipline
185 S. State St., Ste. 1300
Salt Lake City, UT 84111
Phone: 801-531-9110
Fax: 801-531-0660

Client Security Fund
Administrator
Lawyers' Fund for Client Protection
Utah State Bar
645 S. 200 East, Ste. 310
Salt Lake City, UT 84111-3834
Phone: 801-531-9095
Fax: 801-531-0660

Fee Arbitration
Voluntary arbitration
Utah State Bar Fee Arbitration
Coordinator: Maud Thurman
Phone: 801-531-9077
(Address, fax same as
Client Security.)

VERMONT

Attorney Grievance
General Counsel
Professional Conduct Board of the
Supreme Court of Vermont
Office of Bar Counsel
59 Elm St.
Montpelier, VT 05609
Phone: 802-828-3368
Fax: 802-828-3717

Client Security Fund
Executive Director
Vermont Bar Association
35-37 Court St.
P.O. Box 100
Montpelier, VT 05601
Phone: 802-223-2020
Fax: 802-223-1573

Fee Arbitration
Voluntary arbitration
Arbitration of Fee Complaints
Committee
P.O. Box 400
Brandon, VT 05733
Phone: 802-247-3737

VIRGINIA

Attorney Grievance
Bar Counsel
Virginia State Bar
Eighth & Main Bldg.
707 E. Main St., Ste. 1500
Richmond, VA 23219-2803
Phone: 804-775-0500
Fax: 804-775-0501

Client Security Fund
Assistant Executive Director
(Address, fax same as
Attorney Grievance.)
Phone: 804-775-0524

Fee Arbitration
Voluntary arbitration
Refer fee disputes to local bar fee
arbitration programs/committees
Fee Dispute Resolution Program
Coordinator: Carole Tyler
(Address, phone, fax same as
Attorney Grievance.)

VIRGIN ISLANDS

Attorney Grievance
Chairman
Ethics and Grievance Committee
Virgin Islands Bar Association
P.O. Box 6520
St. Thomas, VI 00801
Phone: 809-774-6490
Fax: 809-774-1946

Client Security Fund
None.

Fee Arbitration
None.

WASHINGTON

Attorney Grievance
Chief Disciplinary Counsel
Washington State Bar Association
500 Westin Bldg.
2001 6th Ave.
Seattle, WA 98121-2599
Phone: 206-727-8207
Fax: 206-727-8320

Client Security Fund
General Counsel
(Address, fax same as
Attorney Grievance.)
Phone: 206-727-8232

Fee Arbitration
Voluntary arbitration
Fee Arbitration
Coordinator: Cynthia Jacques
2102 4th Ave., 4th Fl.
Seattle, WA 98121
Phone: 206-727-8275
Fax: 206-727-8320

WEST VIRGINIA

Attorney Grievance
Chief Disciplinary Counsel
Office of Disciplinary Counsel
210 Dickinson St.
Charleston, WV 25301
Phone: 304-558-7999
Fax: 304-558-0831

Client Security Fund
Administrator
2006 Kanawha Blvd., East
Charleston, WV 25311
Phone: 304-558-7993
Fax: 304-558-2467

Fee Arbitration
Voluntary arbitration
Fee Dispute Resolution Program
Coordinator: Thomas Tinder
(Address, phone, fax same as
 Client Security Fund.)

WISCONSIN

Attorney Grievance
Administrator
Board of Attorneys Professional
Responsibility
110 E. Main St., Ste. 410
Madison, WI 53703-3383
Phone: 608-267-7274
Fax: 608-267-1959

Client Security Fund
Legal Services Asst.
State Bar of Wisconsin
P.O. Box 7158
Madison, WI 53707-7158
Phone: 608-257-3838
Fax: 608-257-5502

Fee Arbitration
Voluntary arbitration
Fee Arbitration Program
Coordinator: Kris Wenzel
(Address, phone, fax same as
Client Security Fund.)

WYOMING

Attorney Grievance
Bar Counsel
Wyoming State Bar
P.O. Box 109
Cheyenne, WY 82003-0109
Phone: 307-632-9061
Fax: 307-632-3737

Client Security Fund
Executive Secretary
(Address, phone, fax same as
Attorney Grievance.)

Fee Arbitration
Mandatory arbitration
Committee on Resolution of
Fee Disputes
Coordinator: Tony Lewis
(Address, phone, fax same as
Attorney Grievance.)

WEB SITES

State Bar of Arizona
URL: http://www.azbar.org/disc/disc.htm
Arizona Bar web site features information on fee disputes, the attorney discipline process, when you should file a complaint and how to file a complaint.

State Bar of California
URL: http://www.calbar.org/2con/coninfo.htm
California Bar web site offers information on fee disputes, how to file a complaint against an attorney, an explanation of the complaint process and a downloadable complaint form.

Colorado Bar Association
URL: http://www.cobar.org/publgl.htm
Colorado Bar site offers information on fee arbitration and on who to contact to file a complaint against an attorney.

Kentucky Bar Association
URL: http://www.kybar.org/barcoun.htm
Kentucky Bar features information on who to contact to assist anyone who desires to file a complaint against an attorney for unprofessional or unethical conduct.

Missouri Bar
URL: http://www.mobar.org/sites/mobar/pub/pub-cmpl.htm
Missouri web site features information on fee arbitration and how and when to file a complaint against an attorney.

Nebraska State Bar Association
URL: http://www.nebar.com/caq/disccomp.html
Nebraska State Bar site explains how to file a complaint against an attorney and who to contact with the complaint.

State Bar of New Mexico
URL: http://www.technet.nm.org/sbnm/complain.htm
New Mexico Bar web site features information on fee disputes, the attorney discipline process, when you should file a complaint, and how to file a complaint.

New York State Bar Association
URL: http://www.nysba.org/public/grievance.html
New York State Bar Association web site explains the complaint process, fee conciliation, and who to contact in order to file a complaint against an attorney.

Washington State Bar Association
URL: http://www.wsba.org/discipline.html
Washington State Bar Association site features information on fee arbitration, a summary on the lawyer discipline system, how to file a complaint against an attorney and a downloadable grievance form.

West Virginia State Bar
URL: http://www.wvbar.org/barinfo/services/material.htm
West Virginia Bar's web site offers information how to file a complaint against an attorney.

WEB SITES NOT AFFILIATED WITH THE STATE BAR

Carolina Advocates for Legal Reform (CALR)
URL: http://members.aol.com/CALReform/compl.html
If you have a complaint against a lawyer or judge, or if you have been denied access to the legal system, use the form located on this web site to file your complaint with CALR and the National Complaints Databank.

The Justice Seekers
URL: http://www.divorcedfromjustice.com/
Web site offers a databank where you can add a lawyer's name and tell about your experience with the lawyer - good or bad. Information about lawyers and case situations are available only to members of the web site.

The New Jersey Bartender
URL: http://www.njlp.org/NJbartender.html
"Bartender" web site features a Statewide Attorney Ethics Complaint Roster of New Jersey attorneys that have been disciplined due to complaints filed against them by former clients. Information includes the attorney's name, when the discipline occurred and how the attorney was disciplined. An excellent source to check before you hire an attorney in New Jersey.

6

ALTERNATIVE LEGAL
RESOURCES

This chapter lists some of the latest alternative legal resources available. When you have a legal problem, turning to a traditional lawyer may not be the best answer. Today, you have other options. You can choose from a variety of self-help and low-cost methods of meeting simple legal needs and answering basic questions.

The chapter starts with a list of legal self-help publishers. The best known and largest, Nolo Press of Berkeley, California, offers do-it-yourself and self-help titles, software and kits on subjects ranging from writing a will to filing for bankruptcy. The names of other reputable publishers and the kinds of titles they produce are also included.

We suggest you check the web sites next, even though they are at the end of the chapter, because the Internet is rich with information for legal consumers, including self-help resources, legal research tools, and information and groups that help pro se litigants. Because of space limitations, the sites that are listed represent but a sampling of what can be found on the Internet. New sites are added daily and older sites are often enhanced or updated. Also, the ones we list will probably link you to an abundance of others that offer even more information—the unique capability of the Internet.

The next section we suggest you review is "Advocacy and Support Groups." Depending on the nature of your problem, you may be able to get help, information or a referral from such a group in your area. Most of these are loosely-organized but dedicated groups of activists trying to tackle legal problems or concerns at the local level. Some have a broad focus, while others concentrate on a single issue, such as estate planning or divorce reform.

Next, check out nonlawyer legal service providers, called independent paralegals, as an alternative to hiring an attorney. When all you need is help with a simple or uncontested legal issue, such as incorporating a business, changing your name or filing for an uncontested divorce, one of these low-cost providers may be exactly what you need.

Telephone advice lines are another option: they can let you know about lawyers who try to provide services at greatly reduced prices, especially to self-helpers. Instead of insisting that you hand your entire case over to them, these lawyers have found ways to "unbundle" their services and offer clients a variety of options, so you can buy only what you need. For example, you may want to draft a will or living trust or other basic legal document on your own, but want a lawyer to review it for technical accuracy. Or, you may need someone to answer law-related questions, but don't need representation.

Finally, look into pre-paid legal service plans. These offer a limited list of legal services for a fixed annual fee. Most of them are available only through your workplace as an employee benefit, similar to health insurance, but this section also lists plans that you can enroll in as an individual.

SELF-HELP PUBLISHERS

If you are interested in using do-it-yourself products to handle your legal affairs—books, software, forms and kits —a number of large and small publishers are available to fill your needs. The following list is not exhaustive and does not include major publishing houses that may also carry self-help legal titles.

When using do-it-yourself legal materials, however, it's important to look into the reputation of the company you're dealing with, the expertise of the author who wrote the book, and the copyright date of the product you're buying (to get a sense whether it might be out of date). Ask publishers for an annotated list of their products and prices, something that will go beyond the title to explain what is in the book. Also look into *Books in Print* at your local public library or bookstore for what's available in your subject areas.

A word of caution: Being included in the following list does not constitute a HALT endorsement of the contents.

Allworth Press
10 E. 23rd St.
New York, NY 10010
Phone: 212-777-8395
Fax: 212-777-8261

Legal and other titles that help individuals and small businesses. Subject areas include family law, seniors' rights, estate planning and intellectual property. Also, several titles focus on the legal rights of artists, authors and publishers.

E-Z Legal Forms, Inc.
384 S. Military Trail
Deerfield Beach, FL 33442-3007
Phone: 954-480-8933
Fax: 954-480-8906

Fill-in-the blank legal forms and software. Subject areas include divorce, writing a will or trust and incorporating a business.

HALT, Inc.
1612 K St., NW, Ste. 510
Washington, DC 20006
Phone: 202-887-8255
Toll free: 888-FOR-HALT
Fax: 202-887-9699

Over a dozen self-help titles, including *Using a Lawyer, Probate, Small Claims Court, Using the Law Library, Real Estate, Living and Other Trusts, Everyday Contracts.* Also, the *Everyday Law Series,* a portfolio of answers to commonly asked legal questions.

NOLO Press
950 Parker St.
Berkeley, CA 94710
Phone: 510-549-1976
Toll free: 800-992-6656
Fax: 510-548-5902

A large selection of regularly updated legal forms, books and software. Subject areas include business, finance, estate planning, bankruptcy, family, litigation, intellectual property, small claims and much, much more.

Nova Publishing Company
Small Business and Consumer Legal Publications
1103 W. College St.
Carbondale, IL 62901
Toll free: 800-748-1175

A selection of titles for individuals and small businesses. Subject areas include divorce, wills, incorporation and standard legal forms. Many of the books come with a "Forms-on-Disk" computer disk.

ADVOCACY & SUPPORT ORGANIZATIONS

Legal advocacy and support groups are forming in many communities throughout the nation. Most are local and work at reforming specific aspects of the legal system, such as judicial or lawyer accountability; others work to aid those who have problems with the legal system.

Below is a sampling of these legal groups. The list is not intended to be comprehensive. Check community announcements in your local newspaper or community bulletin boards for meeting information of law-related groups in your area. Many groups also have web sites.

Carolina Advocates for Legal Reform (CALR)
2825 Bancroft St.
Charlotte, NC 28206
Phone: 704-372-9575
Fax: 919-403-5634
URL: http://members.aol.com/CALReform/index.html

CALR, based in Charlotte, NC, works to end the lawyer monopoly over legal services. It helps its members file legal complaints, petitions legislators to initiate legal reforms, and hosts educational workshops and speak-out forums to publicize legal reform.

Consumer Advocates for Legal Justice (CALJustice)
P.O. Box 80716
Las Vegas, NV 89180
Phone: 702-363-5793
URL: http://www.angelfire.com/de/perf/index.html

CALJustice specializes in attorney discipline and general legal reform. It offers information and assistance to people who have problems with lawyers and/or the state bar.

Consumers Coalition of California
1109 Barbara St., Ste. A
Redondo Beach, CA 90277
Phone: 310-316-3346
Fax: 310-316-4115

The coalition acts as a consumers' advocate in hearings with the federal government, in state legislative committees, public hearings, consumer boards of large corporations, and the California Public Utilities Commission. It also intervenes before the California Department of Insurance on legal malpractice problems, and provides mediation services in dealings with state administrative agencies.

Fully Informed Jury Association (FIJA)
P.O. Box 59
Helmville, MT 59843
Phone: 406-793-5550

FIJA is a national organization devoted to educating juries on their right to apply their conscience to deliberations and to veto the law when it believes a just verdict so requires.

Georgia Center for Law in the Public Interest
264 N. Jackson St.
Athens, GA 30601
Phone: 706-546-9008
Fax: 706-546-6481

This group provides legal, educational and technical assistance to grassroots groups in the areas of government accountability and environmental protection.

HALT - An Organization of Americans for Legal Reform
1612 K St., NW, Ste. 510
Washington, DC 20006
Phone: 202-887-8255
Toll free: 888-FOR-HALT
Fax: 202-887-9699
URL: http://www.halt.org/

HALT is dedicated to the principle that all people should be able to handle their legal affairs in a simple, affordable and equitable manner. It works to improve the quality, reduce the cost and increase the accessibility of the civil justice system.

Heirs
P.O. Box 292
Villanova, PA 19085
Phone: 610-527-6260
URL: http://marpleinfo.com/heirs/

Heirs handles the grievances of trust creators and beneficiaries. It works to improve the administration of trusts primarily through education.

Justice Seekers
200 E. 10th St., Ste. 618
New York, NY 10003
URL: http://www.divorcedfromjustice.com/

This grass-roots organization provides information and scrutiny over the judicial practices that characterize the justice system. The Justice Seekers is compiling a databank of lawyer information (good and bad) and offers insights into the family law system.

National Congress for Legal Reform
P.O. Box 214
Huntington Station, NY 11746

Representatives from various legal reform groups throughout the country make up the National Congress for Legal Reform. They work to restore justice, fairness and affordable access to the American legal system.

INDEPENDENT PARALEGALS

You are probably familiar with the term "paralegal." That's a professional who typically works in a lawyer's office or law firm doing legal research, drafting legal documents and helping out in other substantive ways. The work is supervised by an attorney.

But what is an "independent" paralegal? These provide legal services directly to the public, *without* lawyer supervision. They don't have a law degree or a license to practice law, but some have experience working in law firms and some have attended paralegal school. Because they are essentially outside the official legal system and unregulated, no one knows exactly how many independent paralegals are out there helping legal consumers, but some estimate that as many as 5,000 to 10,000 are in business today, mostly in California, Florida, Arizona, Texas and Oregon.

Independent paralegals may specialize in one area, such as bankruptcy or social security, or they may offer a variety of routine legal services, such as basic will preparation, name changes and uncontested divorces. They charge less than lawyers for the same service and often develop a high level of competence in those services simply because they have prepared the same forms so often.

Be aware, however, that independent paralegals are not legally permitted to provide legal advice. For example, they may not tell you what type of will is best for you, or advise you how to complete a will form, or even explain the laws that govern wills. Some independent paralegals stay within these guidelines, but others find it difficult to restrict themselves to distributing forms and filling in the blanks for you without giving advice on how the forms should be filled out. This is particularly true of those who have prepared numerous estate plans. This, in turn, opens them to retribution from state bar associations. It does not, however, mean that any forms you complete under their advice are invalid, if their advice was accurate.

At present, independent paralegals are not organized nationally. Often, state Unauthorized Practice of Law (UPL) rules typically prohibit nonlawyers from practicing law but seldom define what acts constitute "practicing law." Enforcement of these laws is then used to keep nonlawyers, including independent paralegals no matter how well trained, from providing basic legal services. This, of course, keeps costs high and limits your access to the legal system.

Because the field is scattered, largely underground, unregulated and constantly forced to dodge state bar associations that seek to limit the domain of lawyers for lawyers only, there is no good source to go to when you are looking for a good, qualified paralegal to help you handle your basic legal affairs. The best way to find an independent paralegal remains word-of-mouth, searching newspaper advertisements and looking under "paralegals" or "typing services" in your Yellow Pages.

For more information about independent paralegals in California, contact:

California Association of Independent Paralegals (CAIP)
39120 Argonaut Way, Ste. 114
Fremont, CA 94538
Toll free: 800-780-2247

LEGAL TELEPHONE SERVICES

Have you ever had a legal question you wanted answered without spending a lot of money. People with legal questions can get quick information and/or advice through the telephone at costs far below what a lawyer office visit would be.

If you have a legal question, or are a self-helper that needs a little legal advice to proceed, and do not require representation, try calling a legal telephone service.

NATIONAL

Tele-Lawyer

The Tele-Lawyer pay-per-service is available to answer specific legal questions on a legal problem. It is not a referral source for attorneys and Tele-Lawyer will not take on litigation cases or draft documents.

Typical questions for Tele-Lawyer involve family law (divorce, custody and support), landlord-tenant, bankruptcy, Social Security, pensions, taxes and debtor problems, business law, personal injury and criminal law. Tele-Lawyer keeps thousands of legal forms and documents on file which can be faxed or mailed to you.

The staff of attorneys at Tele-Lawyer average over ten years of experience and are licensed in most states. If they are not licensed in your state they will give the general rule, cautioning that it might be different depending on local laws. If they do not know the answer they will terminate the call, research the question and call you back, charging only for the actual time of the two telephone calls. Tele-Lawyer attorneys do not write letters on your behalf, file papers or appear in court.

The Tele-Lawyer service costs $3.00 per minute and the average call is 10 minutes long. When you call Tele-Lawyer, the same strict rules of confidentiality apply as in any other consultation with an attorney.

Tele-Lawyer, Inc.
P.O. Box 110
Huntington Beach, CA 92648
Toll free: 800-TELELAW (billed to your credit card)
Per minute: 900-TELELAW (billed directly to your phone bill)
URL: http://www.telelawyer.com/

LOCAL

Divorce Helpline's California Service Center

The Divorce Helpline employs a team of attorneys that offer legal information, advice and practical problem solving for your California divorce questions. A simple call will allow you to telephone conference with a Divorce Helpline attorney.

Attorneys at The Divorce Helpline average 16 years of experience, are experts in family law, have mediation training and are good at explaining things in plain English. You can get legal information and advice on any divorce-related subject: property, debts, custody, child and spousal support, taxes, practical problem solving, resolution of conflict and how to negotiate with your spouse. You can also set up a 3-person telephone consultation for a additional fee which allows both spouses to speak with a neutral attorney at the same time.

In addition to calling the Helpline, local residents can visit the Service Center which offers document preparation, review of documents prepared by self-helpers and in-office attorney consultations.

Attorney consultations over the phone cost $10.00 per call plus $3.00 per minute billed to your credit card. Call the number below to make a telephone appointment.

Divorce Helpline's California Service Center
2425 Porter St., Ste. 18
Soquel, CA 95073
Toll free: 800-359-7004 (In-State only)
Phone: 408-464-1114
Fax: 408-464-0509
URL: http://www.divorcehelp.com/

PREPAID LEGAL PLANS

Millions of people are enrolled in legal services plans—programs that offer limited services for a set yearly membership fee. Ninety-five percent of them are in "group plans," typically through a professional or trade association, a union or a private employer. These plans are not open to the general public. In group plans, the sponsor (the association, employer or union) may pay all or part of the membership fee.

The remaining 5 percent of participants in prepaid legal services are enrolled in private plans. These are sold directly to individuals through the mail, telemarketing and door-to-door sales. Anyone can join. They are considered *prepaid* because they involve payment of an annual or monthly fee in advance.

The type, size, coverage and cost of these plans vary widely. Some, but not all, also offer litigation services. Most offer the following:

- Unlimited telephone counseling
- Help selecting a lawyer
- Follow-up by telephone and letter
- Document drafting and review
- Reduced rates for any legal representation not included in the membership fee

You may not need to join a plan at all if you're already a member through your workplace or membership in the military, a union, a trade association or nonprofit organization. If you're a senior citizen, you may even be entitled to free legal help (see Chapter 1).

You also probably don't need to join a plan if you rarely need legal advice, or if you already have a lawyer you trust, who is usually available and who charges reasonable fees. You may also want to hold off joining a plan if what you need is immediate legal attention. Your time and resources would be better spent finding the right lawyer or other resource for the job.

Not all plans are created equal. If you decide you would

benefit from joining a prepaid legal plan, you need to evaluate your needs before choosing one, then select the plan that best meets those needs. Call or write for information from the companies listed below, or visit their web sites (for those that have them), then compare what they offer and their annual fees with what you need and are able or willing to pay.

For additional information on legal service plans, contact: **The National Resource Center for Consumers of Legal Services**, P.O. Box 340, Gloucester, VA 23601, (804) 693-9330.

CALDWELL LEGAL, U.S.A.
5464 Ethel Way
P.O. Box 245778
Sacramento, CA 95824-5778
Phone: 916-455-3425
Toll free: 800-222-3035
URL: http://www.caldwell-legal.com/

COUNTRYWIDE PREPAID LEGAL SERVICES
1060 Kings Highway North, Ste. 205
Cherry Hill, NJ 08034
Phone: 609-667-1133

DAWSON LEGAL SERVICES
Pioneer Plaza
900 Fort Street Mall, Ste. 1280
Honolulu, HI 96817
Phone: 808-521-6568

GROUP LEGAL SERVICES, INC.
3737 Camino Del Rio South, Ste. 444
San Diego, CA 92108-4010
Toll free: 800-776-2889

LAWPHONE/ACS
4501 Forbes Blvd.
Lanham, MD 20706
Phone: 301-459-1333
Toll free: 800-255-3352
URL: http://www.lawphone.com/

LEGALINE, INC.
One Securites Center
3490 Piedmont Rd., N.E., Ste.302
Atlanta, GA 30305
Phone: 404-237-7111

LEGALSAVER
Available in California only
Plaza Station
P.O. Box 479
Pasadena, CA 91101
Phone: 818-584-8982

LEGAL SERVICE PLANS, INC.
16 Ann Court
P.O. Box 2405
Meridan, CT 06450
Phone: 203-634-8428
Toll free: 800-772-4577

NATIONAL LEGAL PLAN
330 Motor Pkwy.
Hauppauge, NY 11788
Toll free: 800-292-8063

PRE-PAID LEGAL SERVICES, INC.
P.O. Box 145
Ada, OK 74820
Phone: 405-436-1234
Toll free: 800-654-7757
URL: http://www.pplsi.com/

WEB SITES

SAMPLING OF SELF HELP LEGAL RESOURCES

Allworth Press
URL: http://www.arts-online.com/allworth/home.html
Check here for a full catalog of Allworth materials. Topics include titles on estate planning, seniors, business and the legal rights of artists, authors and publishers.

AV Limited Publications
URL: http://www.avlimited.com/
Site offers previews and prices on about a dozen books and legal kits. Topics include family, estate planning, lawsuit and asset protection and finance. Viewers can also subscribe to "Moneyletter" a montly newsletter dealing with money, law and taxes.

Be Your Own Lawyer Books
URL: http://www.beyourownlawyerbooks.com
Links to over 150 self-help and do-it-yourself legal materials and some state specific books offered online through Amazon books. You can also email legal questions to the lawyer who created this web site.

E-Z Legal Forms, Inc.
URL: http://www.e-zlegal.com
A publisher of books, software and fill-in-the-blank legal forms and kits. Topics range from finance to family to business incorporations. Site includes government, business and legal links.

HALT- An Organization of Americans for Legal Reform
URL: http://www.halt.org/
Library of self-help books available for order by mail, fax, or phone. Provides access to commonly asked legal questions through the *Everyday Law Series* and posts the latest legal reform news.

Nolo Press
URL: http://nolo.com/
One of the oldest and largest do-it-yourself legal book stores. Access to a legal encyclopedia, legal humor, and a huge selection of Nolo and other publishers' books. Over 100 titles available for online purchase. Topics include: the legal system, debt and taxes, financial planning, family and seniors, tenants, legal research, consumer rights, personal injury, insurance, immigration, patents, mediation, malpractice, estate planning and probate, and businesses.

University of Oregon's Law Library
URL: http://www.law.uoregon.edu/resources/law library/sub-index-law.html
Includes links to many legal resources and topics including a link to "Self-Help Legal Resources." Can also conduct legal research online through the University of Oregon's Law Library.

SAMPLING OF LEGAL RESEARCH TOOLS

FindLaw
URL: http://www.findlaw.com/
A fully searchable guide to legal information and web sites on the net. Includes a legal subject index and access to cases and codes, law school information, law reviews, and legal organizations. If your research requires access to judicial opinions, case law, law journals, law reviews, international resources, US government resources, state government resources, library information, legal associations, experts/consultants, law firms, legal news, or law course outlines, you can start by searching this frequently updated site.

Hieros Gamos
URL: http://www.hg.org/hg.html
The largest and only comprehensive legal site with over 20,000 original pages and more than 50,000 links. Site offers information on legal organizations, governments, practice areas, discussion groups, business guides and online seminars.

Internet Legal Resource Guide
URL: http://www.ilrg.com/
Categorized index of 3,100 web sites in 238 nations, islands, and territories. Designed for use by legal scholars and lay persons alike. Searchable categories include: law school rankings, law school course archives, law journals and reviews, news sources, law-related news groups, US federal case law, legal associations, legal experts, and legal forms archives.

LawAid
URL: http://www.lawaid.com/
A database with listings of legal professionals such as attorneys, jury consultants, expert witnesses, etc. Information available on law book publishers and law software.

LawCrawler
URL: http://www.lawcrawler.com/index.html
A comprehensive search engine of legal information on the net. Provides searches of specific countries, international government departments, US code, Federal regulations, Supreme Court and Circuit Court cases, law reviews, legal associations, and law schools.

Law Library Catalogs
URL: http://law.wuacc.edu/washlaw/lawcat/lawcat3m.html
A list of links to law school law libraries accross the country. Offers instructions for telnetting into law school libraries in order to search collections such as those at Cornell and Washburn University.

LawRunner: A Legal Research Tool
URL: http://www.lawrunner.com/
A feature of the Internet Legal Resource Guide, LawRunner provides for the search of the AltaVista™ web index as well as select legal databases. Use LawRunner to limit searches of the AltaVista™ database of 30 million web pages to a particular jurisdiction, or to web sites with a particular domain suffix.

Lectric Law Library
URL: http://www.lectlaw.com/
Offers free legal material for professionals, students,

businesspeople, or anyone interested in law. Organized by rooms, the entire web site is laid out in a user-friendly manner and has a very light-hearted touch. Browse the law dictionary, which the page claims is the biggest on the net, and take a look through the bookstore, which may have the Net's biggest collection of legal software.

University of Oregon's Law Library
URL: http://www.law.uoregon.edu/
Conduct legal research online through the University of Oregon's Law Library. Offers lots of information for the law student, general public and legal profession.

Washburn University Law School and Law Library
Law School: URL: http://lawlib.wuacc.edu/washburn/school.law/wuslw.htm
Library: URL: http://lawlib.wuacc.edu/
Currently one of the best online law libraries. Includes its own navigation system which permits access to U.S Suprme Court opinions through Cornell Law School, all Federal Case law, all Circuit Court of Appeals opinions, U.S. tax code, legislation, Congressional Record, and Code of Federal Regulations.

WestLaw
URL: http://www.westdoc.com/
A databank of full text legal-related documents. Locate documents on the net by citation, docket number, or title (party names). You can retrieve Federal Case law, State Case law, Supreme Court briefs, and more. Both published and unpublished resources are available. Site includes daily law highlights which feature free case summaries.
Note: The retrieval service charges $8.00 to view the text of each document.

SAMPLING OF PRO SE SITES

American Pro Se Association
URL: http://www.legalhelp.org/
Site for a nonprofit, volunteer organization whose mission is to help people with financial and legal problems or questions. Basic information is free to the public, and members have access to Approved Legal Advisors and additional information on various financial and legal subjects.

Divorce Helpline
URL: http://www.divorcehelp.com/
Web site provides information and help with divorce. Site features articles, a directory for the US and Canada of self-help services where you can get a non-adversarial divorce or do it yourself, book store, and forms. Also includes information on their California divorce service center (see page 171).

HOW2
URL: http://www.nolawyer.com/nolawyer/index.html
HOW2 shows you how to protect your right without a lawyer by providing educational law-topic videos, appeal briefs and other documents for those who wish to, or must, represent themselves in Domestic Relations, Juvenile, State Civil, and Federal Civil Rights actions.

Law Made Easy Press
URL: http://laweasy.com/
Web site provides educational and useful online resources for access to legal, tax, estate and financial information. Site features legal planning tips, an interactive planning glossary and other features to help keep you informed.

Legal Strategies Publications
URL: http://www.legalstratpub.com/
Web site contains information that is intended to reduce complex and confusing law to practical general legal strategies. Site features a question and answer forum as well as a legal strategies glossary.

The Pro Se Law Center
URL: http://www.pro-selaw.org/
Web site is a clearinghouse center for collecting research and evaluating reports of pro se approaches to providing access to legal services. Site provides information on cases and materials on pro se litigation, a bibliography of books on self-representation, and links to related sites.

The Self Help Law Center
URL: http://www.selfhelplaw.com/
Site offers information to allow you to make intelligent decisions and preserve your legal rights. Site features law library, custody

and visitation handbook, self-help law books, and an online child support calculator for California residents.

REGIONAL SITES

ARIZONA

Self-Service Center
URL: http://www.maricopa.gov/supcrt/ssc/sschome.html
Web site for the Self-Service Center (program of Supreme Court of Arizona in Maricopa County) which was designed to help people help themselves in court. Site features general information on a variety of topics, court forms and instructions, and lists of lawyers and mediators who will help by providing expert advice.

MARYLAND

Mediate-net
URL: http://www.mediate-net.org/
Maryland's On-Line Mediation Service. This service is designed for Maryland residents who have family law disputes that arise under Maryland law. Site also features information on mediation rules, mediation resources and a directory of family mediators in Maryland.

The People's Law Library of Maryland
URL: http://www.peoples-law.com/
The People's Law Library provides clear explanations of legal subjects, step-by-step procedures, legal forms, and other legal information resources for the citizens of Maryland.

MID-ATLANTIC

Divorce Law Information Center
URL: http://www.divorcelawinfo.com/
The Divorce Law Information Center provides legal information services, and "no-fault" divorce legal form kits to individuals filing their own divorces and other family law actions in Maryland, Virginia, the District of Columbia, and Pennsylvania. Visit the web site for information on other states.

TEXAS

The Law Library of South Texas College of Law
URL: http://www.stcl.edu/library/libgui12.html
Law library site provides a useful list of phone numbers for pro se users.

ADDING INFORMATION
TO DIRECTORY

Send us your recommendations. If you come across a resource that would be helpful to include in *The Legal Resource Directory*, let us know about it. Send us the name of the organization or agency, address, telephone number, contact person and/or web site address and we will investigate it for possible inclusion in upcoming editions of this book. Also feel free to let us know if information about a current listing has been changed so we can update our records.

You can use the form below (a photocopy will do) and send it to HALT.

Contact Person: _____

Organization: _____

Street Address: _____

City: _____ State: _____ Zip: _____

Phone: (   ) _____

Toll Free: (   ) _____

Fax: (   ) _____

URL: _____

Send to: HALT, Inc.
               1612 K St., NW, Ste. 510
               Washington, DC 20006
                  (202) 887-8255
                (202) 887-9699 (fax)
             URL: http://www.halt.org

About HALT

HALT — An Organization of Americans for Legal Reform is a national, non-profit, non-partisan public-interest group of more than 50,000 members. It is dedicated to enabling all people to dispose of their legal affairs simply, affordably and equitably. HALT pursues an ambitious program to improve the quality, reduce the cost and increase the accessibility of the civil legal system.

HALT pursues advocacy at the state and federal levels. In particular, HALT supports:

- Reforming "unauthorized practice of law" (UPL) rules that forbid nonlawyers from handling even routine uncontested matters, limit consumers' options and make legal services unaffordable to many.
- Assuring consumer protection against incompetence and fraud by replacing lawyer self-regulation with public control and accountability in systems for disciplining lawyers and judges.
- Developing standardized do-it-yourself forms and simplified procedures for routine legal matters such as wills, uncontested divorces, trusts and simple bankruptcies.
- Creating pro-consumer alternatives to the tort system, such as alternative-compensation systems that guarantee swift and fair compensation for those injured.

To achieve its educational goals, HALT publishes Citizens Legal Manuals and an "Everyday Law Series"of brief legal guides to increase consumers' ability to handle their own legal affairs and help them become better-informed users of legal services. Written in easy-to-understand language, these materials explain basic legal principles and procedures, including step-by-step "how-to" instructions.

HALT's newsletter, *The Legal Reformer,* is the only national periodical of legal reform news and analysis. It informs readers about major legal reform developments and what they can do to help.

HALT's activities are funded primarily through member contributions.

NOTES

NOTES